PETERSON'S
Holiday Helper

PETERSON'S Holiday Helper

FESTIVE PICK-ME-UPS,
CALM-ME-DOWNS,
AND HANDY HINTS
TO KEEP YOU IN GOOD SPIRITS

Valerie Peterson

CLARKSON POTTER/PUBLISHERS NEW YORK

Copyright © 2008 by Valerie Peterson
All rights reserved.
Published in the United States by Clarkson
Potter/Publishers, an imprint of the Crown
Publishing Group, a division of Random House,
Inc., New York.
www.crownpublishing.com
www.clarksonpotter.com
Clarkson N. Potter is a trademark and Potter
and colophon are registered trademarks of
Random House, Inc.
Library of Congress
Cataloging-in-Publication Data
Peterson, Valerie.
Peterson's holiday helper: festive pick-me-
ups, calm-me-downs, and handy hints to keep
you in good spirits / Valerie Peterson.~1st ed.
Includes index.
1. Cocktails. 2. Holiday cookery. I. Title.
TX951.P4855 2008
641.8'74~dc22
2007041076
ISBN 978-0-307-39546-7
Printed in China
Design by Laura Palese
Ephemera photographs by Paul D'Innocenzo
10 9 8 7 6 5 4 3 2 1
First Edition

FOR "MY SISTERS DEAREST"
LISA & BEVERLY
LOVE & SKÅL!

–CONTENTS–

—INTRODUCTION—

If you're opening this book, you've taken the first step. You've admitted you need **HOLIDAY HELP**.

I was once like you.

All around me were twinkling lights, beautifully decorated trees, gatherings of loved ones, 30-percent-off sales—indications I should be in a jolly mood. After all, when I was a kid, I loved every minute of the season! But as an adult, driven by the many pressures of the holidays, I found myself inexplicably short-tempered with salesclerks, railing at innocent children, kicking over the Salvation Army Santa's bucket. I was told I needed a holiday attitude adjustment.

And, sure enough, during my court-ordered research, it became clear to me that the adults in the celebratory photos of yesteryear looked like they were having a good time, that the children's holiday portraits were taken lovingly by parents who weren't threatening abandonment. From the ancient wassailers to Dickens's Bob Cratchit, from *Miracle on 34th Street's* Mrs. Schellhammer to the memories of my own past, it seemed that adult merriment was actually *possible*, despite the stresses of the season. But how to recapture those blissful holidays of yore? What was the secret?

I searched and searched and, after a whole hour on the Internet, I found the answer: liquor.

Yes, this amazing elixir has historically provided remedial assistance to temper the trials of the season and, I've discovered, taken in various forms, it is just as effective today. It has helped me, and it can help you, too.

A mulled wine will help you steel yourself for inquiries about your now-ex. A spiked cider will help you wash down Grandmama's fruitcake and enable you to tell her it's delicious. A vodka cocktail will help you explain to the children why you've been asked *not* to return to Toys "R" Us.

Of course, there are many soothing panaceas at your disposal. But if you're too distracted by your "to do" list to meditate, if long bubble baths make you wrinkly, if the family doctor is being uncooperative about your refills, look no further. Within these pages you will find liquid pick-me-ups for those predictable holiday hassles and soothing calm-me-downs for those inevitable holiday crises.

Inspired by a wide variety of sources, some recipes are authoritative iterations of time-honored classics, some are refreshingly new. But all these legal (in nearly all states), safe (in moderation) tonics are festive, tasty, and socially acceptable (in most situations; see "Contraindications" for warnings about church services and picking up the kids from school, among other notable exceptions). Most importantly, they have all been developed *to make you merry.*

The book is organized chronologically, from Thanksgiving to the New Year, to take you through the entire season of commonplace, potentially harrowing situations, and to guide you to their liquid solutions. The chapter introductions further elucidate the issues we face during this joyous season, and the sidebars contain additional helpful holiday tips. For easy cross-referencing, a handy "Recipes by Type" guide in the back—sorted by Classics, Hot Drinks, Drinks for a Crowd, Nonalcoholic Drinks, etc.—will further steer you to the recipes for your particular needs.

Whichever drinks you choose to make, be sure to share them with others for maximum efficacy. Mixed and taken as directed, they will keep you and yours in good spirits . . . and then, like me, you will be sincerely wishing peace and goodwill to all.

A Note on THE RECIPES

In an effort to make these recipes as flexible as possible for the holiday host or hostess, I've most often called for a generic type of liquor and occasionally given an example or two of type or brand. However, in the "spirit world" there are a vast number of similarly flavored liquors—especially liqueurs. For example, curaçao, triple sec, Cointreau, and Grand Marnier are all orange-flavored liqueurs. Once you start tasting, you'll notice there's a wide taste—and price—difference among the types and brands.

As blasted luck would have it, the more complex, deeply flavored liqueurs are generally the more expensive ones. In a cocktail with just a few ingredients, the quality of good liquor—Cointreau versus, say, a cheap brand of triple sec—will come through noticeably. The difference is slightly less apparent in a punch or mulled beverage in which there are multiple liquors and fruit juices—or maybe people are just more forgiving when they're availing themselves from a large vat of alcohol. In any event, choose accordingly.

As for the nonalcoholic ingredients, the recipes within call for most to be all natural and unadulterated, rather than presweetened or preflavored juices and mixers (that are often heavier on the sweeteners than on the flavors and/or contain suspicious-sounding chemicals).

You'll taste the difference if your "holiday helpers" are made with 100 percent–real-fruit juices (freshly squeezed, in the case of lemons and limes), homemade simple syrups (quick and easy!), lovingly infused vodkas, and store-bought bitters for that little extra oomph of flavor (all how-to's and handy resources are included).

In the event you have to make a juice substitution, you may need to adjust or omit any sweetener in the recipe, accordingly. For example, if you swap out a cranberry "100 percent juice blend" for the more tart 100 percent cranberry juice called for, be sure to reduce or omit any other sugar or simple syrup in the recipe. Those juice labels can be tricky—read carefully before you mix!

And remember, as tasty as these cocktail recipes are when made as instructed, this book's intention is to make your holidays more enjoyable. Therefore, if any step causes you undue stress, feel free to take whatever shortcuts are necessary to preserve your good cheer.

Whatever way you use these recipes . . . here's to joyous imbibing!

Contra-INDICATIONS

As tasty and festive as they are, there are some situations during which partaking of "holiday helpers" is not considered socially acceptable. Hoisting your flask during church services is generally frowned upon. Throwing back a stiff drink while pregnant might engender dirty looks, among other, more unfortunate consequences. Chugging a cold one while picking up the kids from school might bring round a patrol car (betrayed *again* by those envious PTA moms!). And, speaking of driving, where slightly impaired judgment may help get you through dinner with the extended family—indeed, may have been the stimulus for extending the invitation in the first place—it is a highly inadvisable state in which to operate a moving vehicle. When imbibing, please select a designated driver, and lavish said driver with gifts. He or she is helping preserve your safety during the holiday season as much as the recipes in here might help to preserve your sanity.

1 | THANKSGIVING *lubrications*

PUMPKINS, APPLES, TURKEY, SPICES,

pears, cranberries. The generous bounty of the fall harvest evokes that time of year when we all give thanks for our blessings, for our families . . . and for our favorite distilled beverages.

For many, the fourth Thursday in November is the tip of the holiday ice-cube berg. With this day comes the first seasonal gathering of loved ones, the first traditional sit-down feast, the first family-induced migraine.

The objectives of Thanksgiving Day *seem* simple enough:

1. Express appreciation.
2. Stuff oneself fuller than the bird in the middle of the table.

However, ever since the pilgrims broke bread with the Native Americans, the meal has traditionally brought together people of disparate religious, social, and political beliefs. Add to that the typical elbow-to-elbow seating arrangement of nineteen people at a table meant for eight, and you have a veritable Petri dish for dysfunctional conflict.

It falls to the founder of the feast to deflect conversation away from polarizing topics that might arise—topics such as the torturous horrors inflicted on the poor cage-bred, industrially raised turkey; the unfortunate gastrointestinal side effects of bariatric surgery; who's *really* at fault in the Middle East; or "You didn't tell me you were inviting that worthless brother-in-law of mine!" Should such conversations arise, the host or hostess should help smooth the inevitable rough edges of diverging opinions and, of course, keep the carving knife out of easy reach.

The extraordinary host or hostess, however, will take additional measures to prevent any "perfect storm" conditions that may lead to disharmony. He or she will prearrange the seating and, as with cogs on a wheel, fit the guests together perfectly according to interests and/or keep them apart according to enmities. Then, to minimize friction, he or she will "oil" them with one of the following cocktails—knowing that a moderate dose of soothing balm poured down their throats will help prevent them from going for each other's.

MAYFLOWER MULLED CIDER

"Hey, let's invite those helpful guys down the road, give thanks for not starving to death, and feast for a few days." That fateful gathering in 1621 wouldn't be remembered so fondly if Chief Massasoit and his ninety men showed up *year* after *year*, complaining to the pilgrims that the turkey was dry, or that the Indian corn wasn't prepared just the way they liked it. Luckily, today it's easy enough to reach for the firewater to help "mull" the warm, spicy, seasonal apple cider and keep your own guests plenty grateful.

SERVES *10*

With a potato peeler, peel the oranges and lemon in ¾-inch-wide strips from navel to opposite nib. Reserve the fruit for another use. Stick a clove in each strip of peel. Put the honey, cider, orange peel, lemon peel, and cinnamon sticks into a 4-quart or larger nonreactive saucepan (that is, not aluminum or copper). Warm the mixture over medium-low heat until just simmering, about 20 minutes. Turn heat to low, add the apple brandy, and heat through (do not allow it to simmer after the alcohol has been added). Serve the hot cider in mugs, adding a piece of peel and a dried apple ring to each.

1 large or 2 small oranges

1 large lemon

10 to 15 cloves

½ cup honey

½ gallon (2 quarts) apple cider

3 cinnamon sticks

2 cups (16 ounces) apple brandy, such as Calvados or Apple Jack (see Notes)

10 dried apple rings, for garnish

FAMILY FRIENDLY AND MAKE-AHEAD MAYFLOWER MULLED CIDER:

Omit the apple brandy from the pot. For minors, serve hot cider as is in mugs. For those over 21, place 1 ounce of apple brandy in an individual mug, then fill it with the hot cider mixture. Garnish each with a dried apple ring.

NOTES: Unspiked cider mixture can be stored in the refrigerator for up to a week. When ready to serve, reheat and serve as desired.

TURKEY TAMER

Frozen or fresh-killed? Farm-raised or free-range organic? Roasted or deep-fried? The answers to those perennial Thanksgiving questions matter little, as long as the stressed-out cook remembers to brine. Herself, that is. Toast the beleaguered hostess with a pear-ginger cocktail inspired by the main course, because the turkey is the only one at the table who's made a greater sacrifice than she has.

5 pieces (each about $^1/_2$ inch square) candied ginger (see Note)

2 ounces Wild Turkey (or other bourbon)

1$^1/_2$ ounces pear juice or pear nectar

Place 4 pieces of candied ginger at the bottom of a cocktail shaker. Add the bourbon and muddle (that is, mash the heck out of the ginger) using a wooden spoon or cocktail muddler. Fill the shaker with ice and add the pear juice or nectar. Shake well (until condensation has formed on the outside of the entire shaker), then strain the mixture into a highball glass filled with fresh ice. Garnish with the remaining piece of candied ginger skewered on a cocktail pick.

NOTE: Candied ginger hardens once it's been exposed to air for a while, so you should use it fresh out of the package. If not, chop the ginger first and let it soak a bit in the bourbon to soften.

FLOATING PINK ELEPHANT

Rise at ungodly early hour to ensure prime viewing spot for the children. Practically feel the blood clots forming in legs while waiting for parade to begin. Lose prime viewing spot thirty seconds before parade starts to find Port-o-Potty for the children. Prevent errant child from being trampled by Santa float. When your circulation has been restored, buoy your mood with a lively, cranberry-and-lemon predinner beverage. "Look kids! Look at the giant pink elephant! What? Oh."

SERVES *1*

1½ ounces cranberry-infused vodka (page 119), or 1½ ounces commercial cranberry vodka plus 1 teaspoon 100 percent cranberry juice, for color

1 ounce limoncello

½ ounce freshly squeezed lemon juice

Curl of lemon peel, for garnish

Pour the vodka, limoncello, and lemon juice into an ice-filled shaker. Shake well (until condensation forms on the entire shaker). Strain the mixture into a chilled martini glass. Garnish with the lemon peel.

HOLIDAY TIP

Parade sightline obstructed? Try one of these handy phrases, and then belly right up to the sawhorses:

"Can you believe it? Brad and Angelina, watching the parade from right in the middle of the next block!"

"The doctor told me it's one of those new, antibiotic-resistant forms of TB. Cough. Cough."

"What with getting ready for the holidays and everything, I just haven't had time yet to get everyone de-loused."

THANKSGIVING COOLDOWN

Your brother-in-law, whose very existence defies the notion of "intelligent design," is loudly and vehemently defending the same concept to your neighbor, the Nobel Prize–winning anthropologist. The turkey's internal temperature is still hovering dangerously close to "salmonella" . . . time to serve up a sweet-tart, refreshingly cool distraction.

SERVES *1*

Place the ice cubes in a cocktail shaker; add the cranberry juice, simple syrup, and bitters. Shake well (until condensation forms on the entire shaker). Pour the mixture (including the cranberry ice) into a chilled pint glass. Add the cider. Garnish with a spiral of orange peel.

3 100 percent–cranberry-juice Fruit Juice Ice Cubes (page 121)

2 ounces 100 percent cranberry juice, well chilled

½ ounce Simple Syrup (page 120)

3 dashes orange bitters, such as Fee's

1 12-ounce bottle hard cider, such as Woodpecker, well chilled

Spiral of orange peel

HOLIDAY TIP

To preserve harmony, the following conversation starters are best avoided:

"I liked your *old* nose better."

"*Rejected?* From a *community college?*"

"Look at you! And I'd heard your parole was *denied.*"

"So, where's the little missus been these days?"

PUMPKIN PIE

Dinner is over. The pots and pans are piled four feet high in the sink and your tryptophan-loaded guests are snoring in front of the football game on TV. Who said dessert needed a crust? You've planned ahead and infused for this moment. Shake up a pumpkin-pie-flavored treat, and enjoy the peace while you can. When your company wakes up, they'll all want "a slice," too.

SERVES *1*

2 ounces Pumpkin-and-Spice–Infused Vodka (page 120)

½ ounce Amaretto

1 teaspoon Simple Syrup (page 120)

Cinnamon stick

Fill a cocktail shaker with ice. Add the vodka, Amaretto, and simple syrup. Shake well (until condensation forms on the entire shaker). Strain the mixture into a martini glass. Garnish with a cinnamon stick.

PUMPKIN PIE À LA MODE:

Add 1 ounce of heavy cream and an additional 1 teaspoon of simple syrup before shaking.

CRANBERRY FOG

You *slaved* over the spelt-stuffed Tofurky for your vegan guests, but they're refusing to eat the marshmallow sweet potatoes *and* your signature gelatin mold because—apparently—both dishes are made from horses' hooves. Who knew? Fortunately, the frozen cranberry margaritas you're serving are made from whole, all-natural cranberries and fresh lime juice—and tequila is a vegetable, isn't it?

Place the sugar on a saucer just wider than the glasses. Run the lime wedge around 4 margarita glasses. Dip each glass in the sugar to "rim." In a blender, puree the cranberries, cranberry juice, and simple syrup until the mixture is smooth. Add the lime juice, tequila, orange liqueur, and ice; blend again until smooth. Evenly divide mixture between rimmed margarita glasses and serve.

This can be made a day ahead and stored in the freezer (it will get a bit firm and slushy). Reblend, briefly, to restore drinking consistency.

SERVES 4

- **¼** cup cocktail rimming sugar or granulated sugar
- Lime wedge
- **1** cup frozen cranberries, rinsed (see Note)
- **8** ounces (1 cup) 100 percent cranberry juice
- **4** ounces (½ cup) Simple Syrup (page 120), or more, to taste
- **⅓** cup freshly squeezed lime juice (from about 3–4 limes)
- **8** ounces (1 cup) tequila
- **⅓** cup orange liqueur, such as Cointreau
- **2** cups crushed ice

NOTE: Buy fresh cranberries and throw the bag in the freezer when you get them home from the grocery store.

CORNUCOPIA SANGRIA

You peer into a refrigerator stuffed with leftovers. What can you do with the cold creamed onions, the congealed sweet potato casserole, the not-that-appetizing-even-when-fresh mincemeat pie? You don't have a clue—but you've got a use for that beautiful fruit centerpiece: This cranberry-orange-apple sangria goes *perfectly* with leftover turkey nachos.

Coarsely chop the cranberries in a food processor or by hand, making sure that all of the cranberries have been at least pierced. Place the chopped cranberries and the chunks of orange into a 3-quart or larger pitcher. Add the orange liqueur and muddle the fruit in the liqueur with a cocktail muddler or a wooden spoon to begin to release the juices. Add the apples and mix to blend with the other fruit. Cover and macerate the fruit for at least 2 hours, up to 24 hours. Just before serving, add the chilled wine and the sparkling cider. Stir to mix. Serve in highball glasses, making sure to get some fruit into every serving.

SERVES 8

- **1** cup whole cranberries
- **1** large or 2 small oranges, quartered with peels on, then each quarter cut into 3 pieces to make chunks
- **8** ounces (1 cup) orange liqueur, such as a triple sec
- **2** large or 3 small apples, cored, cut up into $1/2$-inch chunks
- **1** 750-milliliter bottle inexpensive dry red wine, such as rioja, well chilled
- **1** 750-milliliter bottle sparkling cider (such as Martinelli), well chilled

HOLIDAY TIP

Lots of leftovers? Try one of these popular post-Thanksgiving sandwich combos!

THE RETRO
Turkey on buttered white bread, smothered in hot turkey gravy

THE "BACK ON SOUTH BEACH"
Turkey—hold the bread, hold the mayo

THE WORKS
Turkey, stuffing, and cranberry sauce on a Kaiser roll

THE "SOUTH BEACH BACKLASH"
Stuffing, mashed potatoes, and sweet potatoes on a pita

Santa & Me

2 | HOLIDAY
chore chasers

AH, THE MAGIC OF THE HOLIDAYS!

To a child's eye, the tantalizing signs of the season spring forth miraculously as—overnight, it seems—tinseled trees appear everywhere, lights twinkle brilliantly from cozy homes, and the smells of treats waft temptingly from the kitchen. Of course, the climax is Christmas morning, when a multitude of gifts spontaneously generates, the colorfully festive wrapping poised for gleeful shredding.

Yes, to a child's eye, it's all magic. But we of legal drinking age know that, however skillful the sleight of hand, enchantment comes only after much thought, weeks of effort, and at 18¾ percent interest.

To conjure the perfect holiday, decorations need to be dragged down from attics, hauled up from basements, or bulldozed out of ministorage. Trees must be bought and/or assembled and decorated; SUV-loads of gifts must be purchased and hidden; lawn ornaments must be inflated and tethered. Bright wrapping papers, bountiful groceries, and soothing Doan's Pills must be shopped for, schlepped home, and laid in for the duration. Traditional cookies, pies, and cakes must be baked, post office lines must be endured, and family news must be meticulously censored and spun for the annual Holiday Letter.

What's more, like a magician's water-tank trick, seasonal enchantment is fraught with peril for those who hope to create it. Where a child gazes, enraptured, at a twinkling tree, you see hundreds of heat-generating bulbs, plugged in with four extension cords of dubious origins, and know you are enabling a giant fire hazard. Where a tot thrills to the sight of a jolly Santa and his sleigh on the roof, you risk head trauma, a broken back, and almost certain electrocution to mount the twenty-foot ladder while hoisting those eight, not-so-tiny-after-all, light-up reindeer.

Ultimately, the effort and hazards do not deter you—you weather it all to buy, wrap, and decorate your way to holiday delight. And, while you can't wave a wand and be done with it, at least you can shake up one of these tasty, soothing concoctions as a reward for your efforts. They're as close to the magic of the season as you're going to get.

GLÖGG

Experience the self-sufficient satisfaction of cutting your own Christmas tree. Spend hours "hunting" for the perfect coniferous specimen, hack it down, drag it a half mile, and lash it to the car roof. Then ease your back spasms with a traditional Scandinavian restorative that's meant to be shared with a hearty crowd. Just make sure to put away the sharp objects *before* you imbibe.

SERVES 24

1 gallon port wine

1 cup raisins, divided, with $1/2$ cup reserved for garnish

Peel of 1 orange

4 cinnamon sticks

1 tablespoon whole cloves

12 whole cardamom pods, lightly crushed

12 sugar cubes

6 ounces ($3/4$ cup) vodka

24 blanched almonds, for garnish

At least several hours (up to a day) before serving, mix the port, ½ cup of the raisins, the orange peel, cinnamon, cloves, and cardamom pods in a glass or nonreactive (i.e., not aluminum or copper) metal container. Cover and allow to steep in a cool, dry place or in the refrigerator. When ready to serve, place the mixture in a deep, 8-quart, nonreactive pot with a lid. Heat through, but do not boil. Once the mixture is heated thoroughly, turn off the heat and keep the lid at the ready. Place the sugar cubes in a heat-proof, metal strainer over the wine mixture. Pour the vodka over the sugar. Light the sugar, which will flame, with a match; take care and keep face and hands away from the pot. After a few seconds, the surface of the port will flare with a *whoosh*. When the sugar has completely melted through the strainer into the wine, remove the strainer and place the lid on the pot in order to extinguish the flames. Serve in mugs or heat-proof punch cups; garnish each serving with a blanched almond and a few raisins.

HOLIDAY TIP

Having trouble choosing a tree? Here are some common varieties and their relative advantages:

BALSAM FIR: short, flat, rounded needles that are long lasting and less prickly than many other types

DOUGLAS FIR: best fragrance and, generally, best shape

SCOTCH PINE: branches spread best for hanging ornaments; needles stay on even when dry

POLYVINYLCHLORIDE: reusable, flame-retardant, available prewired and/or in colors to match room décor, can be shoved in attic off-season

CHRISTMAS CANDY

Rediscover the simple joys of childhood—the taste of candy canes and chocolate Santas, the piney smell of the tree as you trim it. . . . Try to forget how many calories per ounce are in the candy. Or that Great-grandmama's heirloom glass ornament just crunched under your foot. Just remember one of the simple joys of adulthood—that *cocktails* can come flavored with yummy chocolate and peppermint, too.

SERVES 1

1 candy cane or 4 to 5 red-and-white peppermint hard candies, unwrapped

½ ounce plus 2 ounces clear or white crème de menthe

2 ounces white chocolate liqueur (such as Godiva)

2 teaspoons grenadine syrup (optional, for color)

Put candy cane or candy in a zipper-top bag. On a sturdy cutting board, crush the candy using a heavy, blunt object, such as a rolling pin or mallet, into fine crumbs. Place the candy crumbs in a shallow saucer. Pour ½ ounce of crème de menthe into another shallow saucer. Dip the rim of a martini glass into the crème de menthe, then into the candy-cane crumbs.

Place the white chocolate liqueur, the 2 ounces crème de menthe, and the grenadine (if using) in a shaker with ice. Shake until condensation forms on the outside of the entire shaker, then strain the mixture into the candy-rimmed glass.

We gave ? an old favorite a new twist!

Stik-Ω-pep

STIK·Ω·PEP
LIFE SAVERS

still only 5¢

R~RATED EGGNOG

I saw ELVIS kissing Santa Claus.

The image of the baby Jesus dressed as Elvis was uproariously amusing when the cards were 80 percent off after Christmas last year. Now that you're addressing one to Sister Bernadette, the form-fitting swaddling clothes don't seem like such a good idea. Don't get all shook up: Have a comforting sip of a sweet, creamy, traditional eggnog that's fit for either King.

In a blender, mix the egg substitute, sugar, vanilla, and salt, blend on high until frothy. Add the milk, half-and-half, and rum; blend on low until thoroughly mixed. Serve in punch cups sprinkled with the nutmeg.

NOTE: There's often someone in the crowd who's squeamish about raw eggs. This recipe eliminates any fears, but you can use 4 large whole eggs instead of the egg substitute, if you're not concerned.

G~RATED EGGNOG: Omit the rum.

SERVES 6

12 ounces (1 1/2 cups) egg substitute (available in the dairy case, see Note)

3 tablespoons superfine sugar

1 teaspoon pure vanilla extract

1/4 teaspoon salt

12 ounces (1 1/2 cups) whole milk

6 ounces (3/4 cup) half-and-half

1 cup dark rum (substitute spiced rum, brandy, or other spirits, if you'd like)

Freshly grated nutmeg

HOLIDAY TIP

While Christmas letters are useful for sharing news, it's best to keep them upbeat. Avoid opening sentences such as:

"This year, I got rid of 230 pounds of unwanted fat—my husband."

"At long last, the commitment papers have been signed. . . ."

"As I write this, my ankle monitor chafes . . ."

THE GREEN ELF

Like you told the security guards as they escorted you out of the mall, the manager really overreacted. Sure, the woman may have gotten to that last box before you, but she *plainly* knew that *you saw it first.* And her asking for an ambulance was just *pure* posturing. Before you take out another pesky fellow shopper, take a "time-out" for a revivifying, Grinch-colored, gin-reinforced refreshment.

1½ ounces green apple liqueur

1 ounce gin

½ ounce freshly squeezed lime juice

3 dashes peach bitters, such as Fee's

Pour the green apple liqueur, gin, lime juice, and bitters into a shaker filled with ice. Shake well (until condensation forms on the entire shaker). Strain the mixture into a chilled martini glass.

SPICE COOKIE

Maybe it was because you forgot to buy butter and substituted Golden Harvest Butter-mmm No-Fat Hydrogenated Palm Oil Spread in Great-grandmama's recipe, but the cookies *do* seem rather plasticine and the dog just sniffs and growls at them. But the bake sale must go on—'tis the season of caveat emptor, as they say. While you're packing up the "goodies," sip a little sweet-and-spicy treat of your own.

SERVES *1*

1 ½ ounces cinnamon liqueur, such as Goldschlager

1 ½ ounces spiced rum, such as Captain Morgan

1 tablespoon honey

Pour all of the ingredients into a shaker full of ice. Shake well (until condensation forms on the entire shaker). Strain the mixture into a chilled martini glass.

EMERGENCY GINERATOR

Your neighbor saw your 5,000-watt crèche with the Light-Up Holy Family and raised you Three Luminous-Halo'd Wise Men. You countered by adding the Animated Waving Santa and Nodding Reindeer to your roof; he got the Ho! Ho! Hover-Over-the-House Motion-Sensored Santa Sleigh Track. Before contemplating your next move, relax with a sparkling, ginger-infused refresher and review the inconvenient truth of your kilowatt hours.

SERVES *1*

Pour the gin, syrup, and lime juice into a shaker filled with ice; add the bitters. Shake well (until condensation forms on the entire shaker). Strain the mixture over fresh ice into a tall glass, top with club soda, and garnish with a lime peel.

1 1/2 ounces gin

1 1/2 ounces Ginger-Infused Simple Syrup (page 120)

1 1/2 ounces freshly squeezed lime juice

4 dashes orange bitters, such as Fee's or Regan's

4 ounces (1/2 cup) club soda

Spiral of lime peel

Serve the Coffee that's *Alive* with Flavor!

Nothing you can serve to your family and friends expresses so well the warm hospitality of the season as A&P *premium-quality* Coffee. This fresher, richer coffee is Custom Ground *before your eyes* exactly right for *your* coffeemaker to give you cup after cup of excitingly fragrant coffee that's fairly "alive with flavor." Try it!

EIGHT O'CLOCK COFFEE	RED CIRCLE COFFEE	BOKAR COFFEE
Mild & Mellow	*Rich & Full-Bodied*	*Vigorous & Winey*

GOES WITH CHRISTMAS!

For over 97 years, coffee lovers have found that A&P Coffee just *goes* with Christmas . . . so it's smart to buy the big three-pound bag. Enjoy A&P Custom Ground Coffee in your house, won't you . . . and do have a very *Merry Christmas!*

A&P Custom Ground COFFEE

EXCLUSIVELY AT A&P STORES

More Flavor is why Thousands are changing to A&P Coffee

DOUBLE-STICK SCOTCH COFFEE

It's nearing dawn on Christmas Day and you have only twenty-seven more gifts to go. But you've run out of the "magic transparent" stuff, and so are attempting to seal the packages with a combination of electrical tape and the vintage mucilage you found in the back of your junk drawer. As the sun comes up, spike your morning beverage with a couple of "scotch" potables. They'll help hold *you* together while everyone tears apart your handiwork.

SERVES *1*

1 ounce Drambuie

1 ounce butterscotch schnapps

6 ounces (³/₄ cup) strong, piping hot, freshly brewed coffee

Whipped cream

Butterscotch sauce (optional)

Pour the Drambuie and butterscotch schnapps into an Irish coffee glass or mug. Add the coffee and stir. Garnish with whipped cream and a scant drizzle of butterscotch sauce (if desired).

HOLIDAY TIP

Run out of wrapping paper? Use one of these handy substitutions:

SUNDAY COMICS

ROAD MAPS (make sure to check first with the family driver!)

BROWN PAPER BAGS, ink-stamped with festive holiday designs

DEPARTMENT-STORE SHOPPING BAG, stapled shut, logo covered in seasonally silver duct tape

PAPER TOWELS covered in stickers of colorful, heartfelt drawings made by ailing children, from charity solicitation mailing

3 | *full-of-tradition* "TOASTS"

LIKE THE FERMENTED BEVERAGES

with which we celebrate them, many of our holiday traditions are rooted deeply in the past. The origins of our time-honored decorations, and our festive rituals—such as caroling, gift-giving, storytelling, and the customary foods we cook—are generations, centuries, sometimes millennia old. Some even predate the 1950s.

For example, the evergreen wreath, an ancient emblem of both triumph and eternity, is still hung as a sign of the joyful Christmas season. Each of the eight candles of the Hannukah menorah represents a night the Maccabees' one-day supply of oil miraculously held out. When someone raises a glass to toast the New Year, it's a relic of a time when hosts had to sip first, to prove they weren't poisoning their dinner guests. We still kiss under the mistletoe, a custom that has long associations with "fertility rites," and that, even to this day, is discouraged from being performed with other people's spouses.

Traditional holiday lore and stories can vary widely from culture to culture, but similarities exist. Benevolent figures who bestow gifts, for instance, are a nearly universal Christmas concept. In Italy, the witch Befana—whose shoes are said to be broken from her never-ending search for the Christ child—leaves goodies for well-behaved *bambini* and garlic for the bad. In Scandinavia, children leave porridge for the house-protecting elfin creatures called *tomte* or *nisse*, in exchange for small gifts. In America, kids leave out highly caloric cookies for a jolly cola-advertising icon in exchange for electronic games for the "nice" and fossil fuels for the "naughty."

And although they contain vestiges of the past, traditions don't stand still—they are constantly being modified and adapted for modern times. For example, where once we read a single version of *A Christmas Carol*, we now watch Dickens's classic characters being interpreted by an array of actors ranging from George C. Scott to Vanessa Williams, from Michael Caine to Miss Piggy.

But even in our modern times, as we watch the burning Yule log on DVD, we can still partake of another ancient symbol of light on Earth and the dispersion of human darkness. And, don't you know, a little Wassail Ale or Dickensian Smoking Bishop tastes as good now as it did back when.

HOLIDAY HAND WARMER

Who doesn't root for Fred Gailey to prove that Kris Kringle *is* really Santa Claus? Who doesn't cheer on little Susie Walker while she believes, she believes, it's silly, but she believes? Who doesn't feel just a *touch* of sympathy for that first Macy's Santa when Mrs. Walker takes away his bottle? When you've "gotta do something to keep warm," try this comforting, butter-topped rum classic.

Place the sugar in a mug. Add a bit of the boiling water; stir until the sugar dissolves. Add the rum, then the remaining boiling water. Float a pat of butter on the top; grate nutmeg over the butter.

SERVES *1*

2 teaspoons brown sugar

6 ounces (3/4 cup) boiling water

2 ounces dark rum

2 teaspoons unsalted butter

Freshly grated nutmeg

HOLIDAY TIP

In the mood for a movie? The following classics contain seminal holiday scenes—choose one to go with your particular, season-induced frame of mind.

Nostalgic	Meet Me in St. Louis
Jolly	Elf
Escapist	Holiday Inn
Wishful	Home Alone
Homicidal	Lethal Weapon

WASSAIL ALE

An early precursor to karaoke, "wassailing," somewhat like "caroling," was a quaint custom of trolling the neighborhood in a group, ringing doorbells, and singing good wishes until you were plied with bowls of liquid "good health" (aka "Wass hael"), at which point you went away, leaving the thankful neighbors with a little Peace on Earth.

Place the apples, cider, sugar, ginger, cinnamon, cloves, and nutmeg in a large nonreactive stockpot (that is, don't use aluminum or copper). Bring the mixture to a boil, then turn down the heat, cover, and simmer until the apples become soft, about 20 minutes. Add the ale and heat through, but do not boil (boiling burns off the alcohol). Serve in mugs, giving each person a few pieces of apple.

FOR THE TOAST GARNISH (IF USING): Mix the sugar and cinnamon. Toast the bread. Spread each slice with about 2 teaspoons of the butter; sprinkle with the sugar-cinnamon mixture. Cut each slice in quarters on the diagonal, making 12 triangles in total. Lay a toast triangle across the top of each mug.

SERVES 12

4 apples, cored and chopped into ¹/₂-inch pieces

2 cups (16 ounces) apple cider

¹/₂ cup brown sugar

1 2-inch slice fresh ginger, peeled and chopped into 8 pieces

4 sticks of cinnamon

8 cloves

¹/₂ teaspoon freshly grated nutmeg

6 12-ounce bottles brown ale (such as Newcastle)

TOAST GARNISH (*traditional, but optional*)

¹/₄ cup granulated sugar

1 teaspoon ground cinnamon

3 slices sandwich bread

2 tablespoons butter, softened

THE LUCIALINI

A Sicilian Catholic martyr, Santa Lucia appeared in Sweden in the midst of a winter famine, bringing light and food. There has been speculation that the Swedes were already a little "lit" when they saw the vision, but no matter. On the Feast of Saint Lucy, December 13, stave off the winter darkness in her honor with a bright sparkler made with Swedish lingonberries and Italian Prosecco.

SERVES 1

¾ ounce lingonberry syrup (see "Resources," page 122)

3 dashes orange bitters, such as Fee's or Regan's

5 ounces Prosecco

Strip of orange peel

Pour the lingonberry syrup into a champagne flute; add the bitters. Fill the flute with Prosecco and garnish with the orange peel. Sip and see the light.

ANGEL'S KICK

You'd welcome a little celestial interference to remind you why you were put here—here, in your own home, with an unheavenly host of holiday guests descending on you, all needing three meals a day and clean towels. When it gets to be too much, hole up in your bedroom, kick back, and watch *It's a Wonderful Life*. And, every time a bell rings, have a sip of this vanilla-infused, chocolate treat.

SERVES 1

1 ounce Vanilla-Infused Vodka (page 119) or commercially prepared vanilla-flavored vodka such as Stoli Vanil or Absolut Vanilia

1 ounce dark crème de cacao

1 tablespoon (½ ounce) heavy cream

Cocoa powder, for garnish

Pour the vodka, then the crème de cacao into a 3- or 4-ounce cordial glass. Carefully pour heavy cream over the back of a spoon into the glass, to float a layer on top of the liquors. Sprinkle lightly with cocoa.

DICKENSIAN SMOKING BISHOP

Bah, humbug, you say? Not in the swing of the holidays this year? Well, who wouldn't like a chance to review one's Christmases Past and change a few things—like your high school hairstyle or your choice of a first husband, for example. But skip the ghosts and go right to the spirit-altering beverage that Scrooge offered Bob Cratchit. And God bless us, everyone!

SERVES *8 to 10*

- **5** medium navel oranges, 4 halved crosswise; 1 sliced into 8 to 10 thin rounds, for garnish
- **1** grapefruit, halved crosswise
- **40** cloves
- **½** cup sugar
- **1** 750-milliliter bottle dry red wine (such as cabernet sauvignon)
- **1** 750-milliliter bottle port

Stud the orange and grapefruit halves with 4 cloves each. Use your hands to squeeze the juice from each into a large nonreactive saucepan. Add the spent peels to the saucepan. Sprinkle with the sugar. Over low heat, bring the liquid to a slight simmer; continue to cook for 15 minutes (peels will start to look soft). Turn off the heat and add the wine. Let it steep with the citrus for at least 2 hours or, preferably, overnight in the refrigerator. When ready to serve, strain the wine mixture, again squeezing the citrus halves to extract as much of the liquid as possible. Return the mixture to the saucepan. Add the port and heat through, but do not boil. Serve in mugs, garnished with the reserved orange slices.

STAVE ONE
MARLEY'S GHOST

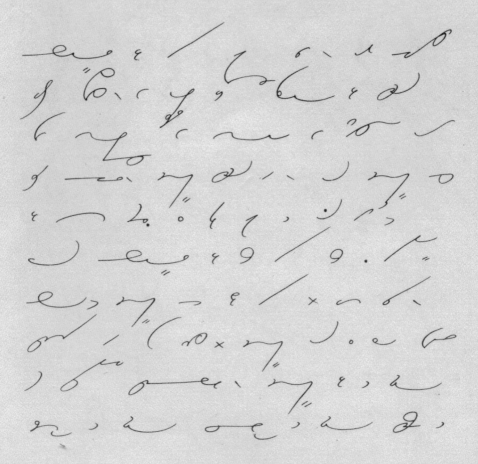

BLACK FOREST

Every year, you dutifully leave carrots for his horse, and every year the German Saint Nicholas reliably leaves you a couple of trinkets. Maybe if you offer up a Black Forest cake–flavored treat—with a kick—he'll finally come through with that plasma TV.

SERVES *1*

2 ounces chocolate liqueur

1 ounce cherry brandy

1 ounce cherry liqueur

½ ounce heavy cream

1 maraschino cherry, for garnish

Pour the chocolate liqueur, cherry brandy, and cherry liqueur into a shaker filled with ice. Shake well (until condensation forms on the entire shaker). Strain the mixture into a rocks glass filled with ice; garnish with the cherry.

HOLIDAY TIP

Tired of wretched excess at the holidays? Start one of these new traditions and better experience the true meaning of the holiday.

Explain to children this year "Santa" is putting a limit on gifts, so he can better serve poor children—have them write their letters accordingly.

Help children thoughtfully choose one of their gifts to donate to the local toy drive.

Forgo shopping altogether, and on Christmas morning pretend "the Grinch" stole all the presents. Patiently explain to sobbing children that Christmas "doesn't come from a store."

THE BLUE GIMEL

You've gone unbeaten three years in a row at the annual family dreidel game—and now that you're all adults, the stakes have been raised to two coins a *put*. While you're tensely waiting to spin, you notice your drink tastes like an orange-y version of the chocolate *gelt*. Which is a good thing, because Bubbe insists on eating the coins out of the pot, so even if you win again, there won't be much left.

Pour the crème de cacao, curaçao, and heavy cream into a shaker filled with ice. Shake well (until condensation forms on the entire shaker). Strain the mixture into a chilled martini glass.

SERVES *1*

2 ounces white crème de cacao.

1½ ounces blue curaçao

½ ounce heavy cream

FRUITCAKE FIZZ

The candied cherries are a color that nature never intended—and they're giving off a faint, kind of eerie glow. You reluctantly take a bite. Tastes pretty good, really, but the texture is kind of weird. What if you took out the cherries but kept the brandy? What if you took out the cake, then added a little fizz? Now *that's* your idea of a treat!

SERVES *1*

- **³/₄** ounce cherry-flavored brandy
- **³/₄** ounce brandy
- **³/₄** ounce freshly squeezed lemon juice
- **1** ounce Simple Syrup (page 120)

  Dash of Angostura bitters
- **2** ounces club soda, well chilled
- **1** green maraschino cherry, for garnish

Pour the cherry-flavored brandy, brandy, lemon juice, and simple syrup into a shaker filled with ice. Shake well (until condensation forms on the entire shaker). Strain the mixture into a highball glass filled with ice. Top with the club soda and stir gently. Garnish with the cherry.

HOLIDAY TIP

Your hostess slaved over her traditional holiday specialty— preserve her feelings by having an excuse at the ready:

"Gosh, I adore *lutefisk*, but my G.I. system is sensitive to anything that's been soaked in lye."

"I wish I'd realized you made your fabulous mincemeat pie—I would've saved room! Can I take my piece home?"

"Thank *God* you told me there are creamed mushrooms in the green bean casserole—I can tell *you* anaphylactic shock is no fun on a holiday."

THE SNUBBED REINDEER

You've been ousted from the annual postdinner Trivial Pursuit game for carelessly leaking answers to the opposing team. There are worse things—remember, better animals than you have been snubbed away from their reindeer games. Come through for your side after all, and elevate their play with a round of chocolatey coffee nips that, in fact, resemble your fellow rejectee.

SERVES 1

1½ ounces coffee liqueur, such as Kahlúa

1½ ounces dark crème de cacao

1 red maraschino cherry

Pour the coffee liqueur and crème de cacao into a sherry glass or other small (3- to 4-ounce) stemmed glass. Float the maraschino cherry "nose" atop the liqueur.

TOM & JERRY

You knew those acting lessons would pay off some-day—the kid's got three more lines than the Virgin Mary! Of course, you have to sit through everyone *else's* amateur thespian efforts but, luckily, the new PTA chair is a genius with the refreshments. Her spirited rendition of the traditional warm Tom & Jerry is more inspired than most of the performances.

Heat the milk on low, until just below the boiling point. While the milk is heating, in a large bowl, beat the egg whites until very stiff; set aside. In another large bowl, beat the egg yolks with sugar and vanilla until thick, light, and creamy yellow. Add the cinnamon, rum, and brandy and continue to beat until thoroughly blended. Fold in the stiffened egg whites and stir or use the beater on the lowest setting and blend just until smooth (there should be about 8 cups of batter). Place batter in a 3-quart punch bowl or decorative Tom & Jerry bowl. To serve, ladle ½ cup batter into mugs or heatproof punch cups. Pour ½ cup of the hot milk into each. Stir, then grate nutmeg on top.

SERVES *16*

½ gallon milk

BATTER

12 eggs, separated

1 cup sugar

2 teapoons vanilla extract

1 teaspoon ground cinnamon

3 cups (24 ounces) rum

1½ cups (12 ounces) brandy

Freshly grated nutmeg, for garnish

NOTES: The batter may separate if made ahead. If this happens, stir gently to remix it before ladling it into the cups.

As an alternative serving method, omit the liquor, then add 1½ ounces rum and ¾ ounce brandy to individual mugs when adding the hot milk.

4 | SOCIALIZING *spirits*

DURING THE FESTIVE SEASON, IT

seems that every familial, social, professional, or religious group to which you belong is hosting a party of some sort, and you are obliged by blood/loyalty/threat of expulsion to attend bearing gifts/a bottle of wine/a covered dish/your grandmother.

With your lengthy list of holiday chores, the inevitable trial and expense of transportation, unpredictable seasonal weather patterns, and the onset of your annual sinus infection, you may be tempted to achieve your holiday joy and laughter alone, hot toddy in hand, while watching *A Charlie Brown Christmas* in your jammies.

But don't give in! Don ye now your gay green/red/plaid/velvet/tree-motif'd apparel and embrace the fact that at the heart of every celebratory season lies . . . *other people*. Since ancient times, traditional gatherings—complete with plenty of holiday mead brewed for the occasion—have provided a way for tribespeople to bond, to help make certain they would be recognized in times of need and assisted with food/shelter/fire/more mead over the long winter, thus ensuring their survival.

In today's fast-paced, socially fragmented world, holiday parties are no less important, helping us to forge deeper connections with, and understanding of, those important to our well-being.

At the office party, while enjoying a cup of punch, you might find yourself finally bonding with your task-master project manager over your respective commuting challenges. At your family dinner, after a glass of wine, your perpetually crotchety great-uncle might tell you his harrowing and poignant emigration story for the first time. At your civic association's fete, you might listen politely as the councilman you voted for, stiff drink in paw, extols the virtues of "swinging" and nude pool parties.

Yes, holiday get-togethers can be invaluable to strengthening the social ties with those around us. But should those ties become uncomfortable, it helps to know that after you've made an appearance, nobody's really going to notice you've gone home to watch Charlie Brown, in your jammies, with your hot toddy.

WKTS Radio
SHEBOYGAN, WIS.   GL 7-5561

4 qts of Whiskey
2 qts of Brandy

and 13 coupled attended
.00 per person = $78.00

BEST ADVERTISING BUY!

Grand Hotel Bill (26)   196 2
Date Dec. 8
M Sheboygan Aldermen
Xmas Party
No.   ACCOUNT FORWARDED
Reg. No.   Clerk

½ Buffet @130	39	00
Diner Room tax	1	17
2	40	17
3		
4	5	10
5	4	00
Soda & Seltzer 6		
Beer Paid 12/10/62 on. 7	4	927
8		27
Plus Tax on Bar 9	49	54
10		
11	4	00
12	53	54
No tip Included. 13		
14 25		
15		

Your account stated to date. If error is found return at once.

LIQUID MISTLETOE

Your boss is slow dancing with the head of Human Resources and your office mate is holed up in the supply closet with the mail boy. How embarrassed they'll all be on Monday! You detachedly survey the bacchanal, sipping the fresh and fruity punch . . . when it suddenly occurs to you that the IT guy is looking mighty sharp today, and that you should go talk to him.

In a punch bowl combine the rum, brandy, orange liqueur, lime juice, and orange juice. Chill until ready to serve. Place the ice ring in the bowl. Add the club soda. Serve in punch cups.

SERVES 30

2 liters dark Jamaican rum, such as Myers

1 liter apricot brandy

1 liter orange liqueur, such as a triple sec

3 cups freshly squeezed lime juice (about 30 limes), well chilled

3 cups orange juice, well chilled

Punch Bowl Ice Ring (page 121)

1 liter club soda, well chilled

HOLIDAY TIP

Not great at remembering names? Fudge your way through the cocktail party with these helpful phrases . . .

"*Pardon* my slip! It's just that you *look* so much like my friend Georgina/my friend George/George Clooney that I got your names mixed up."

"*Wild Man!* How the heck are you?"

"So sorry—ever since my head injury . . ."

NOGINI

Your girlfriends are discussing the total carat weight of their anticipated gifts, and it dawns on you that *your* honey has been dropping phrases like "pounds of suction per square inch." Enjoy a protein- and calcium-rich beverage to strengthen your throwing arm.

Fill a shaker with ice. Add the vodka, Amaretto, half-and-half, egg substitute (if using), and sugar. Shake vigorously until condensation forms on the entire shaker. Strain the drink into a martini glass. Grate nutmeg on top.

SERVES *1*

1 ounce Vanilla-Infused Vodka (page 119), or commercially prepared vanilla-flavored vodka, such as Stoli Vanil or Absolut Vanilia

1 ounce Amaretto

1 ounce half-and-half (or heavy cream)

2 tablespoons egg substitute (optional, but it makes a nice, rich drink!)

½ teaspoon superfine sugar

Freshly ground nutmeg

Christmas Window on the Water Level Route

Watch New York Central trains roll past this time of year. You'll see Christmas windows by the hundred ... bright with the most precious of all gifts. People!

Couples taking their children to see Grandmother (on money-saving Family Fares). Older folk, off to spend Christmas with married sons or daughters—enjoying every minute of New York Central comfort.

Youngsters from school or college getting a first taste of holiday fare in the dining car. Fathers, away on business, taking it easy in the club car ... sure that New York Central will get them home "weather or no."

These are the year's favorite jobs for New York Central men and women. So whether you ride with us or meet the train ... here's wishing you a MERRY CHRISTMAS!

Give Tickets—The Gift that Brings Them Home!
Ask any Central ticket agent how easy it is to send rail and Pullman tickets as your gift to someone you want with you at holiday time.

New York Central
The Water Level Route—You Can Sleep

WHATEVER GETS YOU THROUGH THE WOODS

Whoever said "getting there is half the fun" hasn't traveled in a middle seat in coach with a week's worth of luggage and the seventeen gifts for your extended family, every one of which: 1. weighs over 10 pounds *and* 2. is extremely fragile.

Luckily, you have $10 in exact change to buy the liquor on board—and the flight attendant cooperatively provides the rest of the ingredients, plus ice cubes in a plastic cup.

SERVES 2

Add half each of the rum, the Amaretto, and the orange juice to the plastic cup filled with ice. Squeeze the lime wedge over the mixture, then drop the wedge into the cup. Stir with a metal spoon swiped from First Class. Enjoy with your minuscule bag of dry pretzels. Repeat procedure for the second drink—you'll need both servings.

1 mini bottle (about 1½ ounces) light rum

1 mini bottle (about 1½ ounces) Amaretto

1 can (about 5½–6 ounces) orange juice

2 wedges of lime

HOLIDAY TIP

"The best things come in small packages"—especially when you have to carry them on board. These "diminutive" gifts are always welcome, and easy to transport!

- $100 bill
- Mont Blanc pen
- Classic pearl earrings
- "Cigarette lighter" spy camera
- Pouch of unset diamonds

POINSETTIA

Your neighbor has never been particularly friendly, so you were actually shocked she was having the Open House—until you realized she just redecorated. Vibrantly colored, your classic cocktail is as pretty as it is delicious—but with an all-white living room, she *really* shouldn't be serving red drinks.

Put the cranberry juice, simple syrup, and orange liqueur in a shaker with ice. Shake well (until condensation forms on the entire shaker). Strain the mixture into 6 champagne flutes, pouring an equal amount (about 2½ ounces) into each. Add the champagne, dividing the bottle evenly among the flutes. Garnish each drink with 3 fresh cranberries skewered on a cocktail pick.

SERVES *6*

6 ounces (³/₄ cup) 100 percent cranberry juice

3 ounces Simple Syrup (page 120)

6 ounces (³/₄ cup) orange liqueur, such as Cointreau

1 750-milliliter bottle champagne, well chilled

18 fresh cranberries, for garnish

DARK AND SNOWY

The weather outside is frightful. A freak snowstorm has dumped twenty-three inches in four hours and your eleven dinner guests are now competing loudly for a spot on your pull-out sofa. Hand them all shovels and tell them you'll be the judge. And since *you* have no place to go, fix up a delightful winter riff on a "Dark and Stormy," and let it snow, let it snow, let it snow.

SERVES *1*

- **2** ounces Goslings Dark Seal Rum
- **2** ounces half-and-half
- **1** ounce Ginger-Infused Simple Syrup (page 120)

Pour all the ingredients into a shaker filled with ice. Shake well (until condensation covers the entire shaker). Strain the mixture into a highball glass filled with ice.

FUZZY RED NAVEL

Your brother got a new digital camera, and now the sight of you at 6:30 a.m.—no makeup, in your oldest nightgown, no underwear, *backlit*—is forever immortalized for family viewing. You must trash the image but you know the only way he'll put down his new toy is if you hand him something he likes even better: an antioxidant-enriched, holiday brunch–worthy drink.

SERVES *1*

1 ½ ounces peach schnapps

2 ounces pomegranate juice

4 ounces (¹/₂ cup) orange juice

Orange slice, for garnish

Pour the schnapps and juices into a highball glass filled with ice. Stir; garnish with the orange slice.

NOTE: For a brunch crowd, you can make this by the pitcher using 3 cups (24 ounces) peach schnapps, 1 quart (4 cups) pomegranate juice, and ½ gallon (8 cups) orange juice.

Drink a full BIG glass every day!

Be as good as FLORIDA ORANGE JUICE!

It comes with the gift of golden vitamin C

There once was a time when a good child at Christmas was rewarded with an orange in his stocking—a once-a-year treat so good it stood for goodness. But Florida has taken oranges out of the luxury class. Grows 'em by the million, ships 'em by the train load. Packs their *naturally* sweet juice into handy cans and fresh-frozen concentrate to save Christmas-rushed folks time and trouble.

Christmas morning, *every* morning, get your daily quota of resistance-building vitamin C in a full *big* glass of Florida orange juice. "C" is one vitamin your body doesn't store. You need it every day. *And how* you need it this happy, hectic holiday season!

Florida Fresh-Frozen Concentrate

Pure juice of fully ripe fruit—no sugar added. Year-round source of the flavor and vitamin C of fresh oranges. No fuss, no muss to fix. America's fastest growing family drink.

Florida Canned

Natural full-strength juice, rich in vitamin C. Just open the can and pour! *Blended* orange and grapefruit juice is delicious, too!

Florida Fresh

Thin-skinned—true *juice* oranges, picked and packed just hours ahead of shipping time. Nature's most delicious source of vitamin C. Buy 'em by the bagful. And don't forget—tangerines are back for the holidays. The season's short and sweet. Enjoy 'em while you can.

Florida Oranges

Florida Citrus Commission
Lakeland, Florida

MERRY MOCKTAIL FIZZ

Being relegated to the kids' table has its advantages—for example, nobody minds when you laugh so hard that soda comes out of your nose. But this year you can't help but notice that the "big table" *does* get a more festive beverage selection than the nonalcoholic—though very tasty—one you've been served. Make a note to yourself to inquire about reassignment. After all, you're over twenty-one.

SERVES *1*

2 ounces pomegranate juice

1 ½ ounces Simple Syrup (page 120)

½ ounce freshly squeezed lime juice

Festive Ice Cubes (page 121)

Club soda

Pour the pomegranate juice, simple syrup, and lime juice into a shaker filled with regular ice. Shake well (until condensation forms on the entire shaker). Pour the mixture into a tall glass filled with Festive Ice Cubes. Top with club soda and stir.

HOLIDAY TIP

Table talk with the elderly relatives a little snooze-worthy? This year, try one of these discussion-stimulating comments:

"It was always clear to me that Aunt *Edna* was Grandmama's *favorite.*"

"But I'd heard our *real* great-great-grandpapa was a Cossack."

"You think she went *peacefully*? Doesn't anyone else here watch *Dateline*?"

5 | PRESENT-ATION *potions*

OF ALL THE HOLIDAY TRADITIONS,

gift-giving is arguably the most prevalent. Over the past couple of thousand years, what began as the respectful offering of three kings has become a pan-religion social ritual performed with those nearest and dearest—as well as with everyone from your cubicle mate to your barber, from your PTA committee co-chair to your endermologist.

The questions that dominate the holiday are "To whom?" (are you obligated to buy a Christmas gift for your Buddhist yoga instructor?), "How much?" (what is the appropriate tip for a preschooler's French tutor?), and/or "What?" (you're considering the electric Panini for One for your unmarried sister: Useful appliance? Or bitter reminder?).

And even after you've settled those questions, as you jockey for scarce resources (parking lot space/mall concourse elbow room/limited seating in the food court) and witness displays of road rage/ped rage/interminable-wait-for-sales-help rage, thoughtfulness (looking for their favorite color/favorite scent/favorite licensed character) gives way to desperate "generi-gift" measures (black gloves with gift receipt/Starbucks gift card/cash).

Of course, you *could* consider cutting your list. But do you really want to risk ticking off your postal carrier? Your cleaning lady? Your bikini waxer? You decide "better safe than sorry" and so can't avoid the inevitable last-minute foray to the all-night drugstore to grab a little something for your barista/your mother-in-law's pet schnauzer/your mother-in-law.

When they started all this, maybe the Three Wise Men had to travel through a desert or two, fend off a few thieving infidels. Maybe they had to rely on the occasional oasis, rather than a handy ninety-two-pack of bottled water from Costco. But they didn't have to circle the mall parking garage forty-three times with no star to guide them to an empty space. They didn't have to risk being trampled by their fellow consumers at the Day After Thanksgiving 5:00 a.m. Special Savings Event. *They* had only *one* person to buy for.

As far as gift-giving goes, you've got it much, much rougher. But at least *you* can take a cocktail break—and you'd prefer that to an oasis any day.

MERRY BERRY MOJITO

Although you'd love to buy Clyde in Accounting a stick of Mennen, you've been advised by Human Resources that it *(a)* isn't in keeping with the "goodwill to all" spirit of the holiday and *(b)* may, in fact, be legally actionable. Strangely, your Secret Santa gave you a bottle of mouthwash. He or she should know you only like mint when there's rum involved.

In the bottom of a tall glass, muddle the berries with the lime juice and simple syrup by mashing with a cocktail muddler or a wooden spoon. Add the mint leaves (reserving the small sprig) and bruise the mint with the muddler. Fill the glass with crushed ice; add the rum and stir. Top with club soda (if desired). Garnish with the reserved mint sprig.

SERVES *1*

¹/₂ cup frozen mixed berries, thawed; or fresh, if in season

1 ounce freshly squeezed lime juice

1 ounce Simple Syrup (page 120)

2 large mint sprigs (at least 6 large leaves on each), plus small sprig for garnish

Crushed ice

2 ounces light rum

2 ounces club soda, well chilled (optional)

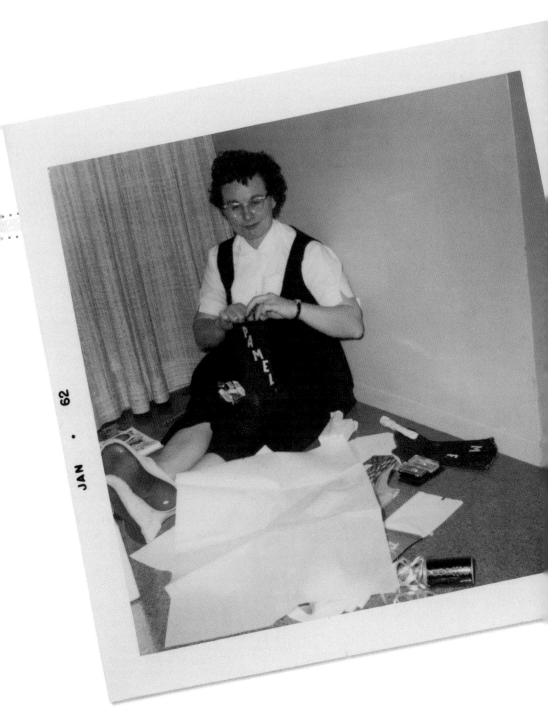

JAN · 62

LICORICE WHIP COAL~AH

Did any of them clean their rooms? Help with the dishes? You've cut them slack up until now, but kids have to learn a lesson sometime. What's the use of *threatening* every year if you never follow through? So fill the stockings, wash the coal off your hands, mix a licorice-tasting cola drink—and prepare yourself for your children's upcoming psychotherapy bills.

SERVES *1*

2 ounces anise-flavored liqueur, such as Sambuca

2 ounces cola

Large wedge of lemon

Pour the anise-flavored liqueur into a highball glass filled with ice. Add the cola; squeeze the lemon wedge over the drink, then drop the wedge into the glass. Stir.

HOLIDAY TIP

Stuck for last-minute stocking stuffers? Here are some items you likely already have handy:

Magazine subscription card with note: "To come!"

Deck of playing cards (preferably new)

Last year's candy canes

Calendar from your favorite charity

Unopened office supplies "borrowed" from place of employment

GINEROUS REGIFT

It's been sitting in your closet for . . . how long now? It really is a true *collector's item*. It's just not the right *color* for your décor. You bet it would fetch a bundle on eBay. . . . Actually, you think you *know* someone who would appreciate it. You finish your second lip-smacking melon-lime cocktail, and now you're sure: Yes, it's *exactly* the kind of thing she'd *love*.

Pour the gin, melon liqueur, lime juice, and bitters into a cocktail shaker filled with ice. Shake well (until condensation forms on the entire shaker). Strain the mixture into a martini glass. Garnish with the lime peel.

SERVES *1*

2 ounces gin

1 ounce green melon liqueur

1 ounce freshly squeezed lime juice

2 dashes Angostura bitters

Curl of lime peel, for garnish

HOLIDAY TIP

Here are a few of the most popular "regifts"— items many will appreciate:

- **Scented candle**
- **Boxed chocolates**
- **Novelty canapé spreaders**
- **Soap-on-a-rope**
- **Holiday-themed "naughty nudie" tie-tack**

NICE 'N' NAUGHTY HOT CHOCOLATE

The kids have asked why it is that Santa's got state-of-the-art surveillance equipment so he'll know at every minute whether they're being "naughty" or "nice," but why he's not technologically savvy enough to accept their Christmas list via text message. Distract them with some hot chocolate for the whole family. Make yours "naughty" with chocolate and coffee liqueurs, and ponder the many mysteries of the season.

SERVES 4

- **½** cup unsweetened cocoa
- **½** cup sugar

  Pinch of salt
- **1** quart (32 ounces) whole milk
- **4** ounces (½ cup) chocolate liqueur, such as Godiva
- **2** ounces (¼ cup) coffee liqueur, such as Kahlúa
- **4** heaping tablespoons Marshmallow Fluff
- **1** 1-ounce piece of a dark chocolate bar

In a 2-quart saucepan over low heat, combine the cocoa, sugar, salt, and about ½ cup of the milk. Stir until well blended and lumps are dissolved. Add the remainder of the milk and turn up heat to medium; heat through until piping hot but not boiling. While the hot chocolate is heating, pour 1 ounce of chocolate liqueur and ½ ounce of coffee liqueur in each of 4 mugs. Add 8 ounces (1 cup) of hot chocolate to each mug and stir. Top with blobs of Marshmallow Fluff. Use a potato peeler to shave a few flakes of chocolate onto each blob.

NICE HOT CHOCOLATE:

Omit the two liqueurs.

HOLIDAY TIP

For Maximum Success, Avoid the Following When Writing Your Letter to Santa:

The phrase "Even though I've been pretty bad this year . . ."

Demands, such as "I have to have . . ." or "I'll die if I don't get . . ."

Any references to past gift disappointments and/or compensation one feels due for such

Thinly veiled threats to reindeers'/elves'/Mrs. Claus's well-being

SANTA'S HELPER SCOTCH HOLIDAY SOUR

The store wanted an extra $50 to put it together, but you know you could assemble it with your eyes closed. Now you suspect they tampered with the package, which has only twenty-three ⅜-inch lug nuts instead of the required twenty-nine, and the manufacturer has annoyingly eliminated written directions in favor of pictographic characters who seem to mock you. Before you're tempted to eat the silica gel, just so you can sue, shake up a cherry-flavored sour named for Santa's tireless helper—*you*.

SERVES *1*

2 ounces Scotch whiskey

1 ounce cherry-flavored brandy

½ ounce sweet vermouth

2 teaspoons Simple Syrup (page 120)

¾ ounce freshly squeezed lemon juice

1 green and 1 red maraschino cherry, for garnish

Pour the scotch, cherry brandy, vermouth, simple syrup, and lemon juice into a shaker filled with ice. Shake well (until condensation forms on the entire shaker). Strain the mixture into a sour glass or a highball glass filled with ice. Garnish with the cherries.

EMERGI-GIFT COFFEE LIQUEUR

Your neighbor arrives at your doorstep with a plate of her hand-dipped chocolates. Since she allows her bull mastiff to soil your lawn every day, you didn't realize the two of you were on gift-giving terms. Luckily, you keep an extra bottle of your own easy-to-make homemade cheer on hand for *just* such emergencies.

MAKES *approximately 3½ quarts*

1½ cups freshly ground coffee (see Notes)

2 cups granulated sugar

3 cups packed dark brown sugar

2 vanilla beans, split and seeds scraped out (you'll use both pods and seeds)

1 1¾-liter bottle vodka (see Notes)

1 cup dark rum

SPECIAL EQUIPMENT:

1-gallon glass jar with an airtight lid and bottles for decanting/giving (see Notes)

Brew the coffee in an automatic drip pot using 3 cups of water (the coffee will be very strong). Pour the coffee into a saucepan; add the sugars and vanilla bean pods and seeds. Cook over medium-low heat until the sugar dissolves; do not boil. Let cool. Pour the sweetened coffee into the glass jar. Add the vodka and rum. Allow the mixture to age for a month (to blend and mellow flavors) in a cool area, away from direct sunlight. Decant into separate bottles for gift-giving (see Notes). The liqueur keeps indefinitely when tightly capped (to minimize exposure to air) and stored in a cool, dry place. The finished liqueur will be a thinner consistency than commercially made coffee liqueurs.

NOTES

Strong coffee roasts are recommended for the deepest flavor; choose one you like to drink.

A midpriced vodka is fine, but the cheapest tend to have a harsher edge—choose accordingly.

You can reuse well-washed liquor or wine bottles as long as they have airtight tops—or see "Resources" (page 122) for other gift-giving container options.

CHRISTMAS CONSOLATION

You've never gotten over the fact that, instead of the puppy you asked for, you got another brother. Although your anger-management issues are now under control, you still feel residual disappointment when he shows up every Christmas. But, since this year he's bearing the fixings for an elegant, delicately flavored champagne cocktail, you think you'll finally let bygones be bygones.

SERVES 6

1 cup fresh raspberries (use frozen if necessary)

1 cup elderflower syrup (see "Resources," page 122)

1 750-milliliter bottle champagne or other white sparkling wine, well chilled

The day before serving, combine the raspberries and the elderflower syrup. Refrigerate, covered, to steep. When serving, divide the berries and steeped syrup evenly among 6 champagne flutes. Top with the chilled champagne.

HOLIDAY TIP

Gifts Your Parents Denied You, But That You Can Buy Yourself on eBay Now That You're All Grown Up:

- Chatty Cathy doll
- Massive quantities of Barbie doll outfits
- Furby
- GI Joe
- Cabbage Patch Kids
- Jarts
- Massive quantities of Beanie Babies
- Cher doll and entire wardrobe of Bob Mackie ensembles
- A *real* pistol

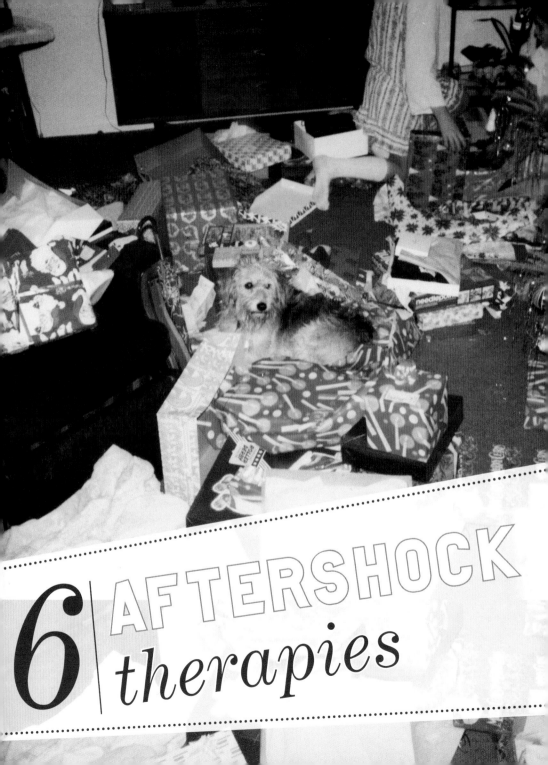

6 | AFTERSHOCK
therapies

THE GIFTS HAVE LONG SINCE BEEN

unwrapped, and half of them still have to go back. The tree is bone dry, drooping like Grandmama without her foundations, and you can't walk on the rug without getting a pine needle embedded between your toes. Leftovers from your holiday repasts jam the refrigerator and you've been slapping together breakfasts of cold roast goose remains, stale snickerdoodles, and/or the anchovies nobody ate from the antipasto tray.

Whether the kids are in your hair, you're dreading the passel of in-laws arriving for your *second* "Christmas" dinner, or it's just that your body craves a return to your preholiday daily ration of fiber/Starbucks/KFC, by now you yearn for a return to some semblance of normalcy.

Unfortunately, that's not going to happen until after the shiny ball drops. So, although the holiday feels as tired as your desiccated fruit basket, remember that these special days won't come around again for a whole year—you should make the best of them. With the preholiday chores behind you—and the dismantling and cleanup not yet begun—why not take the kids skating and relish the additional quality time with family? Why not take advantage of the few days off from work and get those gift returns over with? Why not polish off the chocolate Yule log before the New Year's diet begins?

But after weeks of stresses and chores, even the act of "doing" might be too much. Perhaps the best way to enjoy this "between holiday" time is to just sit with a delicious cocktail for a still, contemplative moment in the dusky, twilit late afternoon of winter. Plug in your tree, put out of your mind that it's shedding six thousand needles an hour, and enjoy the last days of its sparkling, magical twinkle. Instead of wishing life was back to normal, have a sip of your drink and appreciate that you have a few days before you have to go back to work, de-ornament and dismantle the tree, and start your fat-free, alcohol-free diet.

NO SCHOOL SWIZZLE

The kids are off the whole week and they've done nothing but play their new Maximum Mayhem VI: Death & Dismemberment. Helpfully suggest that they amuse themselves with the activities *you* so enjoyed as a child—a jigsaw puzzle or a board game, or perhaps a good book? Have handy this liquid version of "an apple for the teacher" when they laugh you out of the room.

SERVES *1*

- **2** ounces apple brandy
- **³/₄** ounce freshly squeezed lime juice
- **1** teaspoon confectioners' sugar
- **2** dashes Angostura bitters

    Lime slice, for garnish

Pour the apple brandy, lime juice, sugar, and bitters into a tall glass filled with crushed ice. To take out frustrations, "swizzle" by holding a long spoon or swizzle stick between the palms of your hands and rubbing palms together rapidly to mix the drink. Garnish with the slice of lime.

HOLIDAY TIP

Here are some fun games for school break time!

"PUSH THE VACUUM"

OBJECT: Whoever covers the most square footage wins!

PRIZE: Get to keep any loose change found!

BONUS: $5 to whoever finds "Uncle" Jim's wedding ring!

"PLAY OUTSIDE LONGEST"

OBJECT: Stay outside a minimum of 8 hours!

PRIZE: $10!

INSTANT PRIZE FORFEITURE: More than one 5-minute bathroom break.

"QUALITY TIME WITH DADDY"

OBJECT: Locate MIA father by making wistfully plaintive phone inquiries to his usual haunts (gym, pool hall, OTB, etc.)

PRIZE: $25 finder's fee

BONUS: $50 to spend at arcade with Daddy.

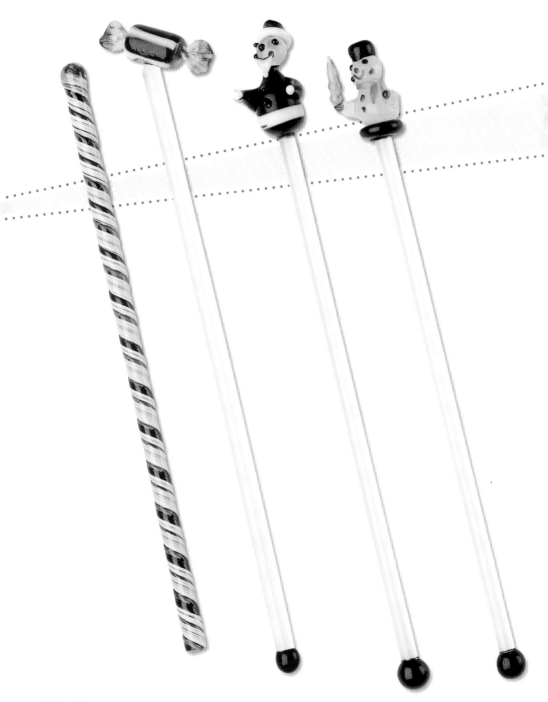

LIQUID LUNCH (HOT BULLSHOT)

A hoard of out-of-town family members is entrenched at your place until New Year's. You choose the lesser of two evils and plead "important project." Luckily, the office is a ghost town this week, allowing you to both play the martyr *and* greatly improve your Spider solitaire score. A drink at lunch might be pushing your luck, but this savory, spiked hot bullshot goes *so* well with your leftover roast beef sandwich.

SERVES *1*

4 to 6 ounces (1/2 to 3/4 cup) hot beef stock or beef bouillon

1 teaspoon freshly squeezed lemon juice

1/2 teaspoon Worcestershire sauce

Dash or more of hot sauce, to taste

2 ounces gin

Salt and freshly ground black pepper to taste

In a large mug, combine the hot bouillon, lemon juice, Worcestershire sauce, hot sauce, and gin. Then add the salt and pepper.

MELTED SNOWMAN

You're a little rusty on the snowman construction, but luckily, the kids are too young to know the difference. You should probably go back outside and mention that adage about "yellow snow" . . . maybe after you fix yourself a (white) snow-colored, chocolate-and-vanilla treat.

Pour the crème de cacao, vodka, and heavy cream into a shaker with a few cubes of ice. Shake well (until condensation forms on the entire shaker). Pour the mixture into a martini glass. Toss in the mini chips.

SERVES 1

1½ ounces white crème de cacao

1 ounce Vanilla-Infused Vodka (page 119), or commercially prepared vanilla vodka, such as Absolut Vanilia or Stoli Vanil

1 ounce heavy cream or half-and-half

6 or 7 mini chocolate chips, for garnish

HOLIDAY TIP

Kids—make your snowperson the envy of the neighborhood with nifty "upgraded" accessories found in miscellaneous drawers and closets:

INSTEAD OF BUTTON EYES: vintage silver dollars

INSTEAD OF TOP HAT: lucky cap with favorite sports team's logo

INSTEAD OF WOOL SCARF: Hermès silk square

INSTEAD OF BROOM: Callaway titanium/fusion golf club

HOT TODDY

Rumor has it that the mother-in-law was a ringer on the 1948 Norwegian Olympic bobsled team and, considering her daredevil moves, you don't doubt it. Despite the swelling and your inability to move your wrist, she insists it isn't actually *fractured*. You use your good hand to access your hip flask—thankfully, you proactively brought along a warm, traditional, whiskey "medicinal."

SERVES *1*

1 ounce blended whiskey, such as Seagram's

1 tablespoon honey

1/4 wedge of lemon

4 ounces (1/4 cup) boiling water

Put the whiskey and honey in a mug. Squeeze lemon juice into the mug, then drop in the wedge as well. Pour the boiling water into the mug and stir until thoroughly mixed.

RETAIL REFRESHER

The department store resembles London after the blitz and you vowed you weren't going to charge another item for at least six months. But after four days of visiting with family, who doesn't need a little retail therapy? Yes, a bright new outfit would be just the thing—perhaps some cruisewear to go with an equally refreshing, tropically flavored tonic.

SERVES *1*

1 ½ ounces dark rum

3 ounces pineapple juice

3 ounces club soda

Wedge of lime ($1/4$ of fruit)

Pineapple chunks, for garnish

Pour the rum and pineapple juice into a tall glass. Fill it with ice; pour in the club soda. Squeeze lime juice into the glass, discard the lime wedge, and stir. Garnish with pineapple chunks skewered on picks.

HOLIDAY TIP

While the post-holiday sale prices might be compelling, avoid buyer's remorse and think twice before you buy such "final sale" items as:

- White, endangered-species-fur-covered ottoman

- "Chinese Language Simplified" 37-disk set

- Designer pants the size you wore in high school

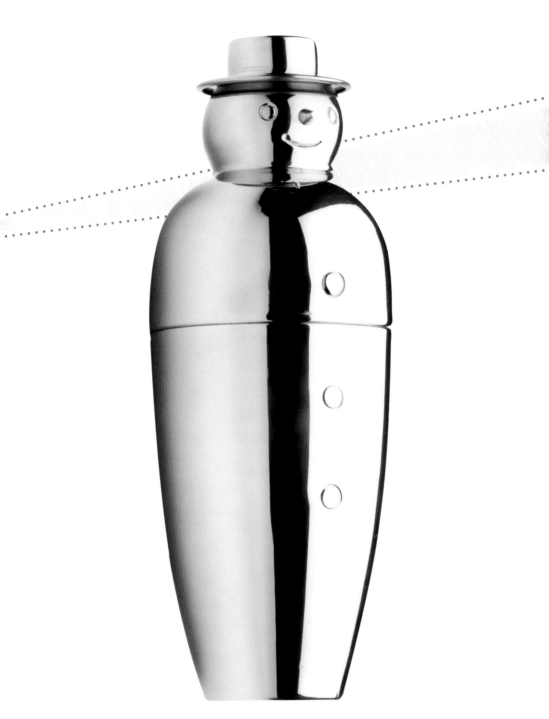

COLD REMEDY

The guy next to you on the plane spent the whole flight trying to hack up a lung, and your visiting niece might as well have been Typhoid Mary for the germs she was spewing at you. No wonder you're coming down with something. Fortify your germ-wracked body with chicken broth, sooth your throat with lemon, and gently ease your suffering with a little vodka.

SERVES *1*

6 ounces (³/4 cup) hot chicken broth

1 teaspoon freshly squeezed lemon juice

¹/2 ounce vodka

Salt and freshly ground black pepper to taste

In a large mug, combine the hot chicken broth, lemon juice, and vodka. Season with salt and pepper. Park yourself, with soup, on the couch. Watch mindless television.

7 | RINGING-IN
refreshments

WHAT HAPPENED TO THOSE RESOLUTIONS

you made last year? You're up ten pounds instead of down twenty. You haven't yet gotten a new job/cheaper car insurance/rock-hard abs, and your diet still lacks fiber. You haven't quit smoking or drinking or gambling or reading *US Weekly*. And, instead of saving for a down payment/beefing up your retirement account/paying off your bookie, you're still spending $15 a day on grande mocha latte-chinos.

But all's not lost: It's almost the New Year.

Since ancient times, the start of a new orbit of the sun has been viewed as an occasion to begin anew, to make right and make way for positive changes in the coming 365 days. People in some early cultures repaid financial debts at the New Year to gain a literal and symbolic fresh start. The agrarian Babylonians, according to some sources, made it a point to return borrowed farming equipment. These practices are no longer customary, which is fortunate for those of us whose credit card debt rivals the GNP of a small country, or who don't remember whose lawnmower is in our garage.

But some traditions *have* persisted. Just as in days of old, New Year's rituals help us expiate the unwanted leftovers of the past. For example, making noise at midnight began as an effort to drive evil spirits from the door at the year's start. In parts of South America, effigies of the old year and mementos of misfortunes are still burned to eradicate any undesirable trace of the previous year. After many a festive New Year's celebration, the practice of "detoxing"—at home or away—helps to purify the body in preparation for a fresh start of good clean living/spiritual enlightenment/the SlimFast plan.

However seemingly superstitious, these practices reinforce our desire to kick habits, drop baggage, and trade in our imperfect selves for much-improved models.

Of course, it is quite possible to bang on pots, burn your "old year," even return your neighbor's lawnmower and still find you've made little progress toward betterment. In that case, it helps to remember that there's nothing wrong with the old you that a little holiday beverage can't cure—or at least make you forget about.

I GET A KICK

When he told you he'd be having something dry and bubbly at midnight, you thought he meant champagne, not beer. But, really, what did you expect from a guy wearing nothing but a New Year Baby diaper? Luckily, one of his friends is more sophisticated, and is assembling stylish, effervescent cocktails with Benedictine and bitters. Too bad he doesn't kiss as well as Mr. PBR.

SERVES 1

1 sugar cube

3 dashes orange bitters, such as Fee's or Regan's

1 ounce Benedictine liqueur

6 ounces (3/4 cup) champagne or other dry sparkling wine

Spiral of orange peel, for garnish

Place the sugar cube in a champagne flute. Add the bitters and Benedictine. Fill the flute with champagne. Garnish with the orange peel.

HOLIDAY TIP

Sparkling wines and punches are the stimulants of sparkling wit—and whopping hangovers. Here are some good, preventative rules to follow:

1. EAT—a full stomach slows the absorption of alcohol.

2. DRINK WATER—before, during, and after drinking—dehydration is a main cause of hangover symptoms.

3. EXERCISE MODERATION—have no more than one standard drink per hour.

4. WRITE tips numbers 1 through 3, above, on your hand: Like all good rules, they're much harder to remember after a few drinks.

MIDNIGHT PUNCH

You caught a glimpse of your reflection in the inky depths of the punch bowl, and immediately made half a dozen more resolutions. But after a few cups of the grapey, crowd-pleasing mixture—well, the New Year is looking pretty bright again.

In a punch bowl, combine the blackberry schnapps, grape juice, and lemon juice. Add the ice ring, and pour in the Lambrusco and club soda. Serve in punch cups.

SERVES 40

1 liter blackberry schnapps

8 cups (½ gallon) purple grape juice, well chilled

4 cups (1 quart) freshly squeezed lemon juice (about 16 lemons), well chilled

Punch Bowl Ice Ring (page 121)

2 liters Lambrusco, well chilled

2 liters club soda, well chilled

HOLIDAY TIP

Here's a tried-and-true method for cleaning the tablecloth/napkins/entire front of your favorite blouse that has been sullied by red wine stains:

Using a rubber band, secure the soiled fabric tautly over a bowl. Hold bowl firmly with one hand; with the other, pour boiling water through the stain from a height of at least a foot.

Here's a tried-and-true method for relieving the scald burns on your hand:

Immediately apply cold water to burn for at least five minutes and up to an hour. If pain persists, take aspirin or acetaminophen—or have a glass of red wine, being careful not to spill.

FORGET-ME-NOT

He's been looking at you kind of funny. Could he be the guy you made out with at last New Year's party? Hmmm. You thought that guy had darker hair. And you don't remember the glasses. But if he's not the guy, then why does he keep looking at you like that? Maybe somebody else here remembers . . . or maybe it'll come back to you after another luscious, cherry-orange creation.

In a blender, place the cherries, simple syrup, and orange liqueur. Puree until the mixture is smooth; you should have about 1 cup. Place the rimming sugar in a small saucer. Run the orange wedge around the rims of 6 champagne glasses; dip the glasses in the sugar to rim them. Put 1 ounce (2 tablespoons) of the cherry mixture in each glass (you may have a little leftover). Fill the glasses with champagne, dividing the bottle evenly among the 6 glasses.

SERVES 6

2 cups frozen red cherries, partially thawed

2 ounces Simple Syrup (page 120)

2 ounces orange liqueur, such as Cointreau

Rimming sugar

Orange wedge

1 750-milliliter bottle champagne or other dry sparkling wine, well chilled

RASPBERRY BALL DROP

It's 11:58, the TV cameras are focused on the ball, and you realize nearly everyone at the party is paired up. The eighty-seven-year-old man from 14D is looking at you a little too eagerly; the hostess is rapidly heading your way with her bachelor brother, who's wearing polyester slacks up to his armpits in a nonironic way. You feign stomach cramps and head into the bathroom—taking two cups of the delicious, double-raspberry, double-wine punch to see you through to the New Year.

SERVES 24

The day before serving, put the raspberries in a bowl and cover them with the raspberry liqueur. Cover and allow to steep overnight in the refrigerator. Just before serving, place the raspberry mixure in a punch bowl, add the ice ring, white wine, and then the sparkling wine. Ladle the drink into champagne flutes, making sure every glass gets a couple of raspberries.

2 pounds fresh or frozen raspberries

1 750-milliliter bottle raspberry liqueur

Punch Bowl Ice Ring (page 121)

3 750-milliliter bottles dry white wine, such as sauvignon blanc, well chilled

3 750-milliliter bottles sparkling wine, well chilled

HOLIDAY TIP

IN ANCIENT BRITAIN, the custom of "First Footing" suggested that for the best luck, the first person to step over the threshold in the New Year should be a tall, healthy, handsome, strapping man. In certain circles, this belief is still widely held, although custom dictates that the man be single as well.

HANGOVER HELPER

Your head is pounding, your stomach is upset—you take a swig of the bitters your Italian friends claim will set you right. Ugh! The cure is worse than the symptoms! You take another gulp. Geez! It's like drinking mouthwash! But then again, it's supposed to be good for you—just one more sip. Hmmm, it's really not bad, once you get used to it. Maybe you'll add a little something ginger-y to help soothe your stomach, too.

SERVES 1

1½ ounces Fernet Branca

1 ounce Ginger-Infused Simple Syrup (page 120)

2 ounces club soda

Wedge of lime

Pour the Fernet Branca and simple syrup into a shaker filled with ice. Shake well (until condensation forms on the entire shaker). Strain the mixture into highball glass filled with fresh ice. Top with the club soda and a squeeze of fresh lime.

HAIR OF THE PIT BULL

Who can be expected to remember little things like what one was doing at midnight? Or if there were fisticuffs involved? Or what those mysterious stains on the living room rug are? Or whose living room it is? HAPPY NEW YEAR! Luckily, this smoky, spicy, vitamin- and antioxidant-rich wake-up call will open the sinuses and make everything just a bit clearer.

In a tall glass, mix all of the ingredients with a long spoon, as best you can, considering. Add ice. Garnish with beans or olives (if using).

HAIRLESS PIT BULL: Omit the vodka. It still has quite a bite.

SERVES 1

- **2** ounces (1/4 cup) vodka
- **6** ounces (3/4 cup) tomato juice
- **1** tablespoon freshly grated horseradish, or 2 tablespoons prepared horseradish
- **1** tablespoon freshly squeezed lemon juice
- **1** teaspoon Worcestershire sauce
- **1/4** teaspoon hot smoked Spanish paprika (*Pimentón de la Vera, picante*)

  Pinch of celery salt

  Pinch of black pepper

  Rick's Picks Mean Beans (see "Resources," page 122), or several green olives skewered on a 4-inch cocktail pick, for garnish

TEA WITH A PUNCH

What sensible person would invite you to a party at practically the crack of dawn on New Year's Day? OK, noon. But they should know after such a late night that you'd be tired! OK, hung over. And they're such good friends, it's not like you can politely refuse. . . . OK, you're dying for a cup of their special-recipe tea-and-whiskey punch.

SERVES 20

4½ cups water

6 berry-flavored tea bags (such as Celestial Seasons Black Cherry Berry)

3 cups blended whiskey, such as Seagram's

3 cups sloe gin

3 cups orange juice, well chilled

1½ cups freshly squeezed lemon juice (about 6 lemons), well chilled

Punch Bowl Ice Ring (page 121)

In a large pot, heat the water until it comes to a rolling boil. Turn off the heat and add the tea bags. Steep them for 20 minutes, then remove the tea bags and cool the tea to room temperature; refrigerate until cold. (The tea can be made up to 2 days ahead; keep it refrigerated.) When ready to serve, place the tea in a punch bowl. Add the whiskey, sloe gin, orange juice, and lemon juice. Stir and add the ice ring.

HOLIDAY TIP

Many cultures believe eating auspicious foods on New Year's Day will bring luck in the coming year.

- Carrot slices symbolize COINS.

- Black-eyed peas and lentils symbolize ABUNDANCE.

- Cabbage leaves and collard greens symbolize GREEN CASH.

* Note that "luck" may also be accompanied by griping stomach pains.

FRESH START

There's time to kill before Power Pilates—you can make some progress on your "classic-book-a-week" resolution. The mail carrier arrives with the confirmation of your French lessons and—drat!—you forgot to cancel your subscription to *People*. Since you've resolved to go green, you *can't* waste a tree. Catch up on celebrity gossip while sipping a nutritious, toxin-clearing beverage with just a touch of vodka. Hey, if it was too healthy, it might send your body into shock.

SERVES *1*

Pour the carrot juice, pomegranate juice, grapefruit juice, prune juice, and vodka into a tall glass filled with ice. Mix well. Garnish with a prune skewered on a carrot stick.

2 ounces carrot juice (beta-carotene)

2 ounces pomegranate juice (antioxidants)

2 ounces grapefruit juice (vitamin C)

2 ounces prune juice (good for what ails you)

1 ounce vodka (flavoring agent)

Prune, for garnish

Carrot stick, for garnish

EPIPHANY

You've dismantled and stowed away the decorations. The relatives have retreated to their respective lairs for the cold-weather months. The last shred of wrapping paper has been vacuumed off the rug, and you've stuck to your digestive cleansing regimen for a whole two days now. Yes, it's good to be back to normal, even if the house looks a little empty without the tree . . .

Hey, look at the January clearance circular! All animated, light-up lawn ornaments are 80 percent off! Maybe you should swing by the store and pick up a couple—it's never too early to be thinking of next year . . . after all, the season will be here again in no time.

And, after having had a little holiday help this year, you're actually looking forward to it.

Basic Recipes AND TECHNIQUES

INFUSED VODKAS

Infusing vodkas couldn't be simpler: vodka + fruit (or herbs) + time = infusion. Be sure to use a glass container and, for these recipes, plan to steep the vodka at least two weeks before using. Midpriced brands of vodka, such as Smirnoff, work fine, but the cheapest brands tend to have a harsh edge. Since infusions are so easy to make, you might want to test different brands before you make a batch for gift-giving. Store infusions in a cool, dark place, away from direct sunlight, or in your freezer. They keep indefinitely once decanted.

cranberry-infused vodka | MAKES 6 cups

1 12-ounce package fresh cranberries (about 3 cups), well rinsed and dried

6 cups vodka

SPECIAL EQUIPMENT:
½-gallon (2-quart) glass jar with airtight lid

Place the cranberries in a jar and pour the vodka over them. Close the lid and let the mixture steep for at least 2 weeks in a cool, dry place, away from direct sunlight. Shake it occasionally. Taste the mixture periodically; when the vodka is to your liking, decant it into clean, airtight bottles, straining out the cranberries and sediment. Store in a cool, dry place or in your freezer indefinitely.

vanilla-infused vodka | MAKES 6 cups

2 whole vanilla beans

6 cups vodka

SPECIAL EQUIPMENT:
½-gallon (2-quart) glass jar with airtight lid

With a sharp knife, split the vanilla beans in half lengthwise. Scrape out the seeds. Place the pods and seeds in the jar, then pour in the vodka. Close the lid and let the mixture steep for at least 2 weeks in a cool, dry place, away from direct sunlight. Shake it occasionally. Taste the mixture periodically; when the vodka is to your liking, decant it into clear, airtight bottles, straining out the pods, seeds, and sediment. Store in a cool, dry place or in your freezer indefinitely.

pumpkin-and-spice–infused vodka | MAKES **approximately 6 cups**

3 cups peeled, cubed, seeded fresh
pumpkin flesh (a 2-pound baking
pumpkin should yield the right amount)

2 sticks of cinnamon

1 vanilla bean

6 cups vodka

SPECIAL EQUIPMENT:
½-gallon (2-quart) glass jar with airtight lid

Place the pumpkin and cinnamon sticks in the jar. Slice the vanilla bean lengthwise; scrape out seeds. Add the seeds and pods to the jar, then pour in the vodka. Close the lid and let the mixture steep for at least 2 weeks in a cool, dry place. Shake it occasionally to mix. After 2 weeks, taste the vodka periodically, until you're happy with the strength of the infusion. At that point, decant the contents into clean, airtight bottles, straining out the pumpkin, spices, and sediment. Store in a cool, dry place or in your freezer indefinitely.

SYRUPS

simple syrup | MAKES 1³⁄₄ cups

1½ cups sugar   **8** ounces (1 cup) water

Place the sugar and water in a small saucepan over medium heat. Bring to a simmer, stirring occasionally until all the sugar dissolves and the mixture is clear. Cool; store in an airtight glass jar for up to 2 weeks in the refrigerator.

ginger-infused simple syrup | MAKES **approximately 1³⁄₄ cups**

1½ cups sugar
8 ounces (1 cup) water

3 3-inch pieces of fresh ginger, peeled and
cut into ½-inch chunks (approximately ¾ cup)

Place the sugar, water, and ginger chunks in a small saucepan over medium heat. Bring to a simmer, lower the heat, and simmer gently for 10 minutes, stirring occasionally. Cool; strain into a glass jar with an airtight lid. The syrup will keep for 2 weeks in the refrigerator.

PUNCH BOWL ICE RING

Ice rings are an ideal way to cool punches, as they melt more slowly than individual cubes. They can be made with plain water, or juices/teas that complement the punch flavorings, which will also minimize dilution. (FYI, alcohol won't freeze—sorry.) To make decorative ice rings, freeze fruit in the middle (described below). In order for the ring to freeze solidly, make sure to start it at least a day or two ahead. Tupperware makes a great ring mold with a removable center for easy release (see "Resources," page 122), but if you don't have a ring mold, use a Bundt pan, or failing that, you can make a square ice block in a thoroughly rinsed half-gallon paper milk carton.

To make a decorative ice ring: Use water or white grape juice, which complements many punches, for these recipes. The ring will freeze relatively transparently, and so show off the fruit. Because fruit tends to float before it's frozen, it's best to freeze in two layers, to get the fruit in "the middle."

Rinse the fruit well. Place the fruit in the ring mold. Pour in the water or white grape juice to fill halfway; freeze until solid. Fill the rest of the mold with the water or juice and freeze until the entire ring is frozen solid.

FOLLOWING ARE SOME SUGGESTIONS FOR DECORATIVE ICE RINGS:

"WREATH": Use 2 cups green grapes, cut into small clusters, and a few scattered cranberries.

CITRUSY: Use slices of orange, lemon, or lime (or a combination), with a maraschino cherry in the center of each.

FESTIVE CRANBERRY: Use 1½ to 2 cups cranberries, scatter with mint leaves.

SPICY: Use spirals of orange peel and cinnamon sticks.

BERRIES: Use 1½ to 2 cups, fresh or frozen.

FESTIVE ICE CUBES

Fill an ice cube tray halfway with water; freeze until firm. Place 1 fresh or frozen cranberry and a mint leaf on top of ice in each individual cube compartment. Pour in water just to cover. Freeze again until firm.

VARIATIONS: *Other berries or citrus fruit rinds can be substituted for cranberry and mint.*

fruit-juice ice cubes

Some recipes call for fruit-juice ice cubes rather than "plain water" ice cubes, in order to minimize diluting the drink's flavor. To make these, pour the recommended juice (cranberry, apple, etc.) into ice cube trays and freeze. Store the frozen juice cubes in a zipper-top bag in the freezer until ready to use. Use any leftovers to chill your favorite nonalcoholic juice drinks.

EQUIPMENT

The following are the most common items you'll need for efficient measuring, mixing, and garnishing. Of course, don't hesitate to improvise if an item isn't handy. As the Petersons say, "Any port in a storm."

BAR SPOON OR ICED TEA SPOON: for stirring and swizzling.

BOTTLE OPENER: for removing bottle tops. Caveat: "Any port in a storm" does not apply to using your teeth for this purpose.

COCKTAIL PICKS: These come in various lengths, and can be plain or thematically decorated. Fancy picks are fun, but toothpicks are a handy substitute.

COCKTAIL SHAKER OR SHAKER SET, INCLUDING STRAINER: for properly blending and chilling cocktail ingredients.

CITRUS REAMER (OR OTHER JUICE-SQUEEZING CONTRAPTION): to extract all that fresh juice you'll be using.

CITRUS ZESTER: for making thin citrus-peel curls.

GLASSWARE: The specific type of glass called for in each recipe generally makes the best presentation, but even a Dixie cup will do in a pinch. For recipes calling for a chilled glass, place the glass in the freezer for fifteen minutes or so before serving.

JIGGER: for measuring 1 to 2 ounces of liquids.

LIQUID AND DRY MEASURING CUPS AND MEASURING SPOONS: for measuring other-than-jigger quantities of liquids and dry ingredients. If you're doing without a jigger, note that 2 tablespoons of liquid equals 1 ounce.

MUDDLER: Usually wood, a muddler is a stick with a flat bottom used for smashing (i.e., "muddling") fruits and herbs to better extract their flavors. If you don't have a muddler, use a wooden spoon.

SAUCERS: small, flat plates on which to spread salt or sugar for use when rimming glasses.

VEGETABLE PEELER: for making wide strips of citrus peel and garnishes, and for making chocolate curls.

WINE OPENER: to decork those wine bottles that don't have screw tops.

RESOURCES

BITTERS: These intense tinctures of many (mostly secret) ingredients add complexity and depth of flavor to cocktails. Angostura Bitters are widely available in supermarkets; Fee's bitters can be found in gourmet shops and at feebrothers.com; Buffalotrace.com sells Regan's Orange Bitters. From their home page, click on "gift shop" and enter "bitters" in the search field.

COCKTAIL OR RIMMING SUGARS: Bevmo.com has a wide selection of just about anything bar related; enter "cocktail sugars" in the search field to find a selection of rimming sugars.

FRUIT SYRUPS: Hafi brand Lingonberry Syrup and Hafi brand Elderflower Drink Concentrate are available at IKEA stores. Other brands, including D'Alba and Bottlegreen, are available in many gourmet food shops, including Olsen's Scandinavian Foods at www.scandinavianfoods.net.

GLASS JARS AND BOTTLES: Although any clean, airtight glass jar will do for your infusions, www.infused-vodka.com has a large selection of fancy-schmancy ones with spigots for serving, and sells stands to display your infusing creations. Housewares stores often sell individual bottles suitable for gift-giving; www.ebottles.com is a source for larger quantities of bottles in many sizes and shapes.

ICE RING MOLD: Available from www.tupperware.com—it's called a Jel-Ring mold.

RICK'S PICKS MEAN BEANS: They're generally available at Whole Foods, or by mail order at www.rickspicks.com.

ACKNOWLEDGMENTS

For the genesis of this book I am indebted to Beverly Peterson, who coined the term "holiday helper" while we fortified ourselves before a family get-together; and to my agent, Jen Griffin, who took the idea a leap further and extorted the book proposal from me.

Thanks to Lauren Shakely and Doris Cooper for welcoming me into their illustrious company at Clarkson Potter. I was blessed to have worked with Amy Pierpont, whose expert editorial hand tuned every note in the manuscript, and I am still blessed with Lindsay Miller, who shepherded the project to completion with the sharp mind of an editor and the careful soul of a writer.

Marysarah Quinn, Jane Treuhaft, and the production folks indulged me my art program; the brilliant Laura Palese elevated it with her wonderful design. Paul D'Innocenzo masterfully shot any piece of holiday flotsam I handed him with the utmost care; Pam Yosh and John Connelly generously snapped Pam's fabulous vintage barware.

I'm grateful for the marketing, publicity, and special sales dream team, including Sydney Webber, Katherine Sungarian, Kate Tyler, and Jean McCall, who enthusiastically embraced the project from its earliest stages. Whatever was being served at that first meeting, I want the recipe. . . . And to the Random House sales folks—especially Jaci Updike, Al Greco, and Christian Waters—shout-outs from "the dark side"!

My heartfelt appreciation goes out to all those people who steered me to/procured/entrusted me with cherished family photos/collectibles/recipes/their own images. Those pictured within are noted with page numbers: Bill Charron (pp. 82, 102); Helen Charron (p. 102); Anne Cipolla (pp. 60, 114); Gregory Citarella (p. 88); Lynn Citarella (p. 96—shout-out to Bill Barthels!); "Pop" Citarella and Pussy Cat (p. 100); Maureen Daly; Patricia Donahue (aka "Patsy Holland," p. 93); Anna Dunn (p. 80); Jimmy, Mary, and Tommy Dunn (p. 84); Mr. and Mrs. Thomas Dunn (pp. 80, 106); Nancy Egan (p. 82); Libby Forlano; Marc Frattasio (author of *Dining on the Shore Line Route*); Janice Fryer; Mildred Fryer (p. 74); Steve Karchin and Gary Kraut at Alphaville; Andrea Kochman; Jean Latona (p. 60, 114); Bob, Brent, Marc, and Pat Laymon (p. 68); Elizabeth Lyngholm; Helen Lyngholm (p. 94); Meredith McGuiness; Esther McSpedon; Lorraine McSpedon; Jerry Nixon at Mr. Pink; Eileen O'Neill (pp. 31, 48); Marion O'Neill (pp. 60, 72, 114); Michael O'Neill (p. 48); Annie and Eddie Parsells; Janie and Eddie Peterson; Anna "Farmor" Peterson (p. 6); Beverly Peterson (pp. 5, 38, 93); Lisa Peterson (pp. 5, 14, 38, 93); Robert Peterson (p. 5); Rowena Peterson (p. 16); Louisa Pricoli; Carolyn Rostkowski (p. 18); Audrey and Steven Rostkowski; Karin and Jim Sedgwick; Eleanor Tedeschi; Michael Tisdale; Mary Beth Thomas (p. 54); Eileen Vaughn (p. 82); and Pam Yosh (p. 18).

Cheers to my "everyday helpers"—including my taste testers (who, oddly, always liked the third drink best): Kitt Allan, Barbara Alpert, Rose Arlia, Inga-Lena Bengtssen, the Birkelands, all members of the Block Island Cocktail Research Institute, Susan Callahan and the tasters at her sunset party, Geoffrey Dampeer, Scott Dare, Linda Dickey, Sarah Durand, the Firstenbergs, Sharon Gamboa, Marge Ginsburg, Liz Harwell, Tina Hill, Ingrid Kasper, Jolene and Brian Kennedy, the Klings, David Latt, Emily Loose, Maryann Manelski, Tina McCormick, Mary Alice Mullen, Amy Nover, Erica Okone, and the tasters at her Long Beach bash; Gail O'Rourke, the Petersons (especially Laura), Judy San Gregorio, Keith Pfeffer, Christoper Phillips, the Santinis, the Smiths, Mike Spoto and the guys at Bleecker Court, the Towers, and Diane Weingarten.

For their generous assistance with the Byzantine world of permissions, I'm grateful to Marjorie Anders, Karen Copley, Linda Friend, Vivien Galiano, Dominique Giammarino, Sara Griffith, Craig Grybowski (Go A&P!), Paul Klein, Alissa Kleinman, Claudia Poll, Scott Russo, David J. Schuman, Kelly Scotti, Joan Shedlovsky, Kathleen Sheldon, Nancy Slivoski, and Diana Zaremba.

And for priceless inspiration, thanks to my tireless holiday hosts, especially Richard and Carol; Arlene and Mike; Anne Marie and Richie; Eileen, Vinny, and Dale; Mary, Carl, and Gail; and Mom and Dad.

CREDITS & PERMISSIONS

Pages 9, 10, 11, 22, 30, 32, 34, 35, 40, 42–45, 49, 52–53, 55, 56, 64, 70, 76, 90, 98, 104, 116 by Paul D'Innocenzo; page 2,3 © 1960 by Wilsonart International, Inc., reprinted with permission; pages 5, 12, 14, 16, 38, 65, 86, 93: R. Peterson family collection; page 6: McSpedon family collection; page 18, Santa Float: Rostkowski family collection; page 18 (cocktail tray), 21 by Pam Yosh/John Connelly; pages 28, 88, 96, 100: Citarella family collection; page 31 © 1951 by Lifesavers, Wm. Wrigley Jr. Company, reprinted with permission; pages 33, 48, 60, 72 and 114: O'Neill family collection; page 34 © 1937 by Church & Dwight Co., Inc., reprinted with permission of Church & Dwight Co., Inc.; page 36 © 1955 by The Great Atlantic & Pacific Tea Company and The Eight O'Clock Coffee Company, reprinted with permission; page 47 © by The Gregg Publishing Company, reprinted with acknowledgment of McGraw-Hill Companies; page 50 © 1963 by Blue Diamond Growers, reprinted with permission; page 54: Thomas family collection; page 67 © 1953 by Florida Citrus Commission, reprinted with permission; page 68: Laymon family collection; page 74: Fryer family collection; page 78 © 1936 by BAKER'S Chocolate, BAKER'S is a registered trademark of KF Holdings and is used with permission; page 80, 84, 106: Dunn family collection; pages 82, 102: Daly/Charron family collection; page 94: Lyngholm family collection; pages 62, 108: Marc J. Frattasio collection; page 110 © 1965 by The Beistle Company, reprinted with permission.

RECIPES BY TYPE

CLASSICS AND ADAPTATIONS

BLACK FOREST

CORNUCOPIA SANGRIA
(cranberry apple sangria)

CRANBERRY FOG
(Frozen Cranberry Margarita)

DICKENSIAN SMOKING BISHOP
(mulled wine)

GLÖGG

HAIR OF THE PIT BULL
(Hot and Smoky Bloody Mary)

HOLIDAY HAND WARMER
(hot buttered rum)

HOT TODDY

LIQUID LUNCH
(Hot Bullshot)

MAYFLOWER MULLED CIDER

MERRY BERRY MOJITO

NICE 'N' NAUGHTY HOT CHOCOLATE

POINSETTIA

R-RATED EGGNOG

SANTA'S HELPER SCOTCH HOLIDAY SOUR

TOM & JERRY

WASSAIL ALE

DRINKS BY LIQUOR

Ale
WASSAIL ALE
(brown ale)

Amaretto
WHATEVER GETS YOU THROUGH THE WOODS
(light rum, Amaretto)

NOGINI
(vanilla-infused vodka, Amaretto)

PUMPKIN PIE
(pumpkin-and-spice–infused vodka, Amaretto)

PUMPKIN PIE A LA MODE
(pumpkin-and-spice–infused vodka, Amaretto)

Apple Brandy
MAYFLOWER MULLED CIDER
(apple brandy)

NO SCHOOL SWIZZLE
(apple brandy)

Apricot Schnapps
LIQUID MISTLETOE
(rum, apricot schnapps, triple sec)

Benedictine
I GET A KICK
(champagne, Benedictine)

Blackberry Schnapps
MIDNIGHT PUNCH
(lambrusco, blackberry schnapps)

Blue Curaçao
THE BLUE GIMEL
(white crème de cacao, blue curaçao)

Bourbon
TURKEY TAMER
(bourbon)

Brandy
FRUITCAKE FIZZ
(cherry-flavored brandy, brandy)

TOM & JERRY
(brandy)

Butterscotch Schnapps
DOUBLE-STICK SCOTCH COFFEE
(Drambuie, butterscotch schnapps)

Cherry liqueur/Cherry brandy
BLACK FOREST
(crème de cacao, cherry liqueur, cherry brandy)

FRUITCAKE FIZZ
(cherry-flavored brandy, brandy)

SANTA'S HELPER SCOTCH HOLIDAY SOUR
(Scotch, sweet vermouth, cherry brandy)

Cinnamon Liqueur
SPICE COOKIE
(cinnamon liqueur, spiced rum)

Coffee Liqueur
NICE 'N' NAUGHTY HOT CHOCOLATE
(chocolate liqueur, coffee liqueur)

THE SNUBBED REINDEER
(coffee liqueur, dark crème de cacao)

Crème de Cacao or Chocolate Liqueur
ANGEL'S KICK
(vanilla-infused vodka, dark crème de cacao)

BLACK FOREST
(crème de cacao, cherry liqueur, cherry brandy)

THE BLUE GIMEL
(white crème de cacao, blue curaçao)

CHRISTMAS CANDY
(crème de menthe, white chocolate liqueur)

MELTED SNOWMAN
(white crème de cacao, vanilla-infused vodka)

NICE 'N' NAUGHTY HOT CHOCOLATE
(chocolate liqueur, coffee liqueur)

THE SNUBBED REINDEER
(coffee liqueur, dark crème de cacao)

Crème de Menthe
CHRISTMAS CANDY
(crème de menthe, white chocolate liqueur)

Drambuie
DOUBLE-STICK SCOTCH COFFEE
(Drambuie, butterscotch schnapps)

Fernet Branca
HANGOVER HELPER
(Fernet Branca)

Gin
EMERGENCY GINERATOR
(gin)

GINEROUS REGIFT
(gin, melon liqueur)

THE GREEN ELF
(green apple liqueur, gin)

LIQUID LUNCH
(gin)

Green Apple Liqueur
THE GREEN ELF
(green apple liqueur, gin)

Hard Cider
THANKSGIVING COOLDOWN
(hard cider)

Limoncello
FLOATING PINK ELEPHANT
(Cranberry-infused vodka, limoncello)

Melon Liqueur
GINEROUS REGIFT
(gin, melon liqueur)

Orange Liqueur
(see also Blue Curaçao)

CORNUCOPIA SANGRIA
(red wine, triple sec, sparkling cider)

CRANBERRY FOG
(Frozen Cranberry Margarita)
(tequila, orange liqueur)

FORGET-ME-NOT
(champagne, Cointreau)

LIQUID MISTLETOE
(rum, apricot schnapps, triple sec)

POINSETTIA
(champagne, Cointreau)

Peach Schnapps
FUZZY RED NAVEL
(peach schnapps)

Raspberry Liqueur
RASPBERRY BALL DROP
(raspberry liqueur, white wine, sparkling wine)

Rum
DARK AND SNOWY
(Goslings rum)

HOLIDAY HAND WARMER
(rum)

LIQUID MISTLETOE
(rum, apricot schnapps, triple sec)

MERRY BERRY MOJITO
(light rum)

RETAIL REFRESHER
(dark rum)

R-RATED EGGNOG
(rum)

SPICE COOKIE
(cinnamon liqueur, spiced rum)

WHATEVER GETS YOU THROUGH THE WOODS
(light rum, amaretto)

Sambuca/Licorice-flavored Liqueur
LICORICE WHIP COAL-AH
(Sambuca)

Scotch
SANTA'S HELPER SCOTCH HOLIDAY SOUR
(Scotch, sweet vermouth, cherry brandy)

Sloe Gin
TEA WITH A PUNCH
(whiskey, sloe gin)

Sparkling Wines
CHRISTMAS CONSOLATION
(champagne)

FORGET-ME-NOT
(champagne, Cointreau)

I GET A KICK
(champagne, Benedictine)

LUCIALINI
(prosecco)

POINSETTIA
(champagne, Cointreau)

RASPBERRY BALL DROP
(sparkling wine, white wine, raspberry liqueur)

Sweet Vermouth
SANTA'S HELPER SCOTCH HOLIDAY SOUR
(Scotch, sweet vermouth, cherry brandy)

Tequila
CRANBERRY FOG
(Frozen Cranberry Margarita)
(tequila, orange liqueur)

Vodka & Flavored Vodkas
ANGEL'S KICK
(vanilla-infused vodka, dark crème de cacao)

COLD REMEDY
(vodka)

FLOATING PINK ELEPHANT
(cranberry-infused vodka, limoncello)

FRESH START
(vodka)

GLÖGG
(port wine, vodka)

HAIR OF THE PIT BULL
(Hot and Smoky Bloody Mary)
(vodka)

MELTED SNOWMAN
(white crème de cacao, vanilla-infused vodka)

NOGINI
(vanilla-infused vodka, Amaretto)

PUMPKIN PIE
(pumpkin-and-spice–infused vodka, Amaretto)

PUMPKIN PIE À LA MODE
(pumpkin-and-spice–infused vodka, Amaretto)

Whiskey
HOT TODDY
(whiskey)

TEA WITH A PUNCH
(whiskey, sloe gin)

Wine
CORNUCOPIA SANGRIA
(red wine, orange liqueur)

DICKENSIAN SMOKING BISHOP
(red wine)

GLÖGG
(vodka, port wine)

MIDNIGHT PUNCH
(lambrusco, blackberry schnapps)

RASBERRY BALL DROP
(raspberry liqueur, white wine, sparkling wine)

HOT DRINKS

COLD REMEDY

DICKENSIAN SMOKING BISHOP
(mulled wine)

DOUBLE-STICK SCOTCH COFFEE

GLÖGG

HOLIDAY HAND WARMER
(hot buttered rum)

HOT TODDY

LIQUID LUNCH
(Hot Bullshot)

MAYFLOWER MULLED CIDER

NICE HOT CHOCOLATE

NICE 'N' NAUGHTY HOT CHOCOLATE

TOM & JERRY

WASSAIL ALE

DRINKS FOR A CROWD

CORNUCOPIA SANGRIA
(cranberry apple sangria)

DICKENSIAN SMOKING BISHOP
(mulled wine)

GLÖGG

FUZZY RED NAVEL

LIQUID MISTLETOE

MAYFLOWER MULLED CIDER

MIDNIGHT PUNCH

RASPBERRY BALL DROP

TEA WITH A PUNCH

TOM & JERRY

WASSAIL ALE

HOMEMADE

CRANBERRY-INFUSED VODKA

GINGER-INFUSED SIMPLE SYRUP

EMERGI-GIFT COFFEE LIQUEUR

PUMPKIN-AND-SPICE–INFUSED VODKA

SIMPLE SYRUP

VANILLA-INFUSED VODKA

NON-ALCOHOLIC DRINKS

FAMILY-FRIENDLY MAYFLOWER MULLED CIDER

G-RATED EGGNOG

HAIRLESS PIT BULL
(Hot and Smoky Virgin Mary)

MERRY MOCKTAIL FIZZ

NICE HOT CHOCOLATE

SPARKLERS

CHRISTMAS CONSOLATION

FORGET-ME-NOT

I GET A KICK

THE LUCIALINI

POINSETTIA

RASPBERRY BALL DROP